The Collector's Encyclopedia of
NIPPON PORCELAIN

Second Series

by Joan F. Van Patten

COLLECTOR BOOKS

A Division of Schroeder Publishing Co., Inc.

Searching For A Publisher?

We are always looking for knowledgeable people considered to be experts within their fields. If you feel that there is a real need for a book on your collectible subject and have a large comprehensive collection, contact Collector Books.

Additional copies of this book may be ordered from:

Collector Books
P.O. Box 3009
Paducah, Kentucky 42002-3009

@$24.95. Add $2.00 for postage and handling.

Copyright: Joan Van Patten, 1982
Values Updated, 1997

This book or any part thereof may not be reproduced without the written consent of the author and publisher.

**Dedicated to
my parents and my daughters**

ACKNOWLEDGEMENTS

It's been said that bees accomplish nothing unless they work together and neither do people! Series II is the joint effort of a number of notable collectors and authorities on Nippon and the author is indebted to each and everyone.

Marie Young photographed many of the items shown in the book and a number of pieces in her collection are also pictured. Together we visited the homes of Jean Cole and Rita Gillis and were overwhelmed! We literally camped on both of their door steps and they never seemed to tire of our visits and questions. Marie has done a fine job in photographing their lovely items and readers are sure to enjoy seeing these fine collectibles which are shown throughout the book.

To Ken and Leola Harman who graciously sent me photos of so many of their favorite items, thank you so much. They have made a wonderful contribution to the book. Hours were spent by them preparing for photos and writing descriptions and they deserve a special thank you.

Wilf Pegg and Jan Dorlan from Canada provided me with many beautiful photos of their collection. They tell me "Nipponing" is more difficult in Canada but you could never tell it by the items they have managed to collect! Thank you so much.

A number of Syde Zwern's collection of dolls were also photographed and Linda Lau sent several photos of her favorite dolls and miniatures. Including those from my collection we have approximately 125 in the book. I am sure these will prove to be interesting to both Nippon and doll collectors. Again my thanks to these two collectors.

Joan and Dale Waring are two more who spent a lot of time having pictures taken and sending along descriptions to me. They have amassed some truly great finds and I am proud to have had them join the team.

Roger Zeefe has managed to locate some spectacular pieces of Nippon over the years and he was kind enough to photograph many of them to share with our readers. Thank you, Roger.

Jess Berry and Gary Graves made a big contribution with so many of their excellent pictures. Thanks to them Nippon collectors will be treated to seeing some very special pieces.

Virginia and Hank Richardson have also sent many exceptional photos of their collection. Virginia specializes in plaques but has also purchased many other fine items which she has shared with us. Thank you both!

Others I would like to thank who either sent photos or helped with research are:
Sharlene Floam
Bernard and Francine Golden
Corrine Gould
JoAnn Hansens
Joseph Hudgins
Joyce Nelson
Fannie Young
Michael Young

Other photographers I would like to acknowledge and thank are Frank Berning, Wright Bell, Kenneth Harman, Jr., Leola Harman, Wilf Pegg, David Messick, Stuart Floam and Roger Zeefe. Black Studios of Schenectady, NY prepared the cover photo which I am very proud of.

Also my thanks go to Noritake Co., especially Yuki Kato, Assistant to the President, the RCA Co. and the Campbell Co. for their kind help and assistance.

Again my gratitude to those who assisted with pricing which is always difficult, Jean and Craig Cole, Rita Gillis, Marie Young, Wilf Pegg and Roger Zeefe.

And what good is a manuscript and photos without an understanding publisher and one I am proud to be associated with. Thank you Bill Schroeder and your wonderful staff, especially Steve Quertermous for all your help and support.

This book has been the work of many dedicated collectors for the use of other collectors and dealers and a generous thank you to each and every person who became a part of this project. It could not have become a reality without you! But more than just the realization of Series II thank you for the enthusiasm, kindness and friendship you have shown to me during this time.

TABLE OF CONTENTS

INTRODUCTION

The dictionary describes metamorphosis as a "complete transformation of character" and so it is that Nippon porcelain has undergone its own metamorphosis. Just a few years ago, as early as 1970, pieces could be purchased for a pittance. In fact, most dealers would happily sell off a boxful for a few dollars just to get the items out of their shop.

Not so today, for Nippon has found its deserved place with all the other fine pieces of china such as R.S. Prussia, Beleek, etc. And in case you haven't been watching, the prices have been skyrocketing along with its popularity. From cocoon to beautiful butterfly best describes this Nippon event.

Collectors and dealers from all over have finally "discovered" it and although Nippon is not that scarce it may seem to be to an eager collector with a modest budget. Because of this no possible source should be overlooked, grandmother's cabinets, garage sales, even thrift shops. Browse through flea markets, read the advertising in collector publications and visit as many shows as possible. Who knows where or when a "find" may be made.

Some find Nippon overpriced, others find it a bargain, but the fact is prices are forced upward each year by the number of new collectors and an educated guess is that this number has doubled in the last two to three years.

Choice items are becoming harder to find. Collectors that have them know they have something good and have become reluctant to sell which in turn makes those wanting them all the more anxious to buy and prices are soaring. It's a case of the "haves" versus the "have nots" and now some pieces have become almost "untouchable".

The prices seem to be setting themselves. A large profit may be made immediately if one has the right contacts and is able to buy low and sell high but it's often necessary to hold onto an item a year or two to realize a substantial gain. Most buy because of their love of Nippon and my advice for those trying to double their money quickly would be to "fold over your money once and put it in your pocket". That's always a sure way!

What does the future hold for Nippon collectors? Every new record sale brings more buyers stampeding into the market but collectors will always find that the best investment is quality merchandise.

Desirability is influenced by a number of factors, rarity of design and rarity of and CONDITION of the item. But don't fall for the myth "if it's rare, it's always valuable". If no one else wants it it's of little monetary value as popularity plays a big part in the pricing game.

Presently ornate Nippon is fetching fancy prices along with the ever popular relief molded, tapestry, wedgwood, cobalt, portrait and novelty pieces.

There is a wide range of Nippon available but many collectors find themselves limiting their items to specific categories. Most, in fact, are constantly upgrading their collections. Beginning collectors usually buy small, more inexpensive items and then as they gain experience their "wants" generally change.

Remember, knowledge is power and newspaper and magazine ads and antique show prices are all weather vanes for trends. Regional tastes and preferences also play a part in this but it is necessary to keep abreast of what's happening in the market place.

The Nippon market has remained strong the last few years and I believe we have only seen "the tip of the iceberg". Prices will continue to escalate at a quick pace but buyers will become more selective and knowledgeable in their purchases.

Beginning collectors would do well to get to know other collectors and also to visit antique shops and dealers. Experiment, start with something that appeals to you. Study and handle the items. Learn all you can about Nippon but most of all buy because you love the piece of Nippon. Keep abreast of changing tastes and trends and do not make snap judgments on new things, give them the benefit of doubt. Read a lot, ask questions and look for quality. Buy the best you can as the highest quality items will always hold their own.

Many novice collectors buy any and every piece within reach of their pocketbook but it would be wiser for them to be more selective in their purchases.

Truly great collections require work, knowledge and discipline. Also *patience*! They do not happen overnight. There is a big difference between having an accumulation of Nippon and a "collection" of Nippon. An accumulation is merely a hodge podge of items, a mixture collected with little rhyme or reason often just for quantity. The "true" collector, however, doesn't collect just to collect for quantity, but has a purpose in mind along with an eye for quality.

Since the Nippon market is continually changing and new information constantly surfacing it was necessary to expand "The Encyclopedia" to be a two volume set. The second series edition is intended to be a continuation of the first book. New information is included, also additional marks and most important of all detailed data about Nippon reproductions now flooding the market.

Readers will find basic information and photos of color plates numbered 1-366 in the first book. Each book has been designed for the use of the novice collector, occasional dabbler as well as the advanced collector and hopefully these two volumes of "The Encyclopedia" will become a passport to the wonderful world of collecting Nippon.

DETECTION OF DAMAGE AND RESTORATION

Ever get a piece of Nippon home only to discover a crack or hairline? Most of us are quick to buy and quick to trust when the person offering the piece tells us it is in "mint condition".

LOOKING BEFORE YOU LEAP is good advice. Buy quality and always buy the best you can afford for these items will hold their value. Knowingly buying damaged or restored items is a matter that should be left to each collector's judgment. It's rare that these pieces will escalate in value and such purchases should probably be avoided unless the article is extremely rare or very, very cheap. However, there is really nothing wrong in buying either as long as it is always identified as such and not misrepresented.

Know your dealer or else be very careful with your purchase. Never buy an item under poor lighting conditions, always hold the piece up to the light. You can often tell by touching the items if something is wrong. Check the most vulnerable places, areas that project, such as spouts, handles, rims, sprigged-on decoration, etc.

Gold wears off the quickest because it is the last to be fired and it is quite common to find touched-up gold. It is often duller than the original and this fact can often detect its presence. Droplets of color are another tell-tale clue along with pieces of lint or hair which would never have survived firing in the kiln. Check to see if there are any conspicuous areas of dull coloring where surrounding areas are shiny and vice versa. Anyone can be an innocent buyer and be fooled.

Some collectors have approached the problem of detecting hidden damage with the purchase of a long wave ultraviolet light. It can be a valuable aid in the detection of *most* repairs. When viewed under black light, hard to see cracks will fluoresce brightly. And then there are still those who advertise restorations that are invisible under black light. It can really make a collector leary.

RECORDING AND INSURING YOUR COLLECTION

One thing every serious collector should do is keep accurate records on all items. This can be just for your own pleasure but more realistically as a help in case of fire or theft. Three sets should be kept, one at home, one in a safety deposit box and one with your insurance company.

These records can either be kept in book form or perhaps a filing card system could be utilized. Several books for this purpose are already on the market and should be considered by collectors. Photos are a must! Along with these one should list the date and place the item was acquired, original cost and its physical description such as height, width, diameter, etc. Condition should be noted, example: mint, chipped, worn gold, hairlines. The identifying mark should also be jotted down along with the current value of the item. These records should be updated yearly.

Insurance costs always seem to be on the rise as is the possibility of theft. One solution for the collector would be to contain the collection to one that is small and choice. Easy to say, hard to do, so if you are like most who have been bitten by the collecting bug contact your insurance company as to the possibility of obtaining a fine arts policy. It is a rider to the homeowner's policy and since insurance laws vary from state to state it would be advisable to speak with your local agent. Insure the items for their full value. Any new increases in value are not covered so amend your policy periodically. Household accidents such as breakage are not included however.

No one likes to think about thefts and fires but they do occur. First of all do not advertise the existence of your collection to everyone you meet. Good locks on doors and windows are a first step while many other collectors have preferred to install alarm systems. Check with your insurance company as these installations may give you a break on your premium.

NIPPON REPRODUCTIONS

It was bound to happen! Whenever an item becomes popular and zooms in price someone will make an imitation. A large share of the antique business is now being sustained by reproductions which are perfectly all right if they are sold as that. It's when unscrupulous people enter the picture that these pieces prove to be a nightmare for collectors. My quarrel is not so much with the manufacturer or importer but the middlemen in between trying to make a quick but dishonest dollar for many are knowingly misrepresenting the reproductions as genuine "Nippon" era pieces.

Nippon reproductions are turning up with greater frequency and can be found from coast to coast. Shows, auctions, flea markets, no place is immune. The inside of many pieces are rough to the touch and the edges are often unglazed. The fake pieces even have a "Nippon" mark under the glaze. In addition each piece originally comes with a small adhesive backed label giving the country of origin which says Made in Japan. However, after purchase this label can be easily removed and the item can then be "pawned" off to unsuspecting customers as authentic Nippon. This is confusing to beginning collectors and dealers who do not specialize in Nippon. Hence the vicious cycle begins and the pieces are sold over and over again.

One pattern is described in an importer's catalog as "wild flower" and all kinds of items may be purchased, from chocolate sets to covered boxes to footed trinket boxes. Outside edges of these pieces are highlighted with gold paint and the items are medium to light olive green in color and have pink to lavender flower blossoms as the decoration. The items are definitely not Nippon era pieces but merely backstamped Nippon. They have been recently manufactured in Japan and are now being distributed in the United States. The mark found on the "wild flower" items is similar to the M in wreath mark but instead it features an hourglass figure in the middle.

The other known pattern is called "green mist" and has a bisque finish with a light to medium green background. Pink flowers and gold trim decorate the pieces. These items are reminiscent of Limoges items. The mark on these is similar to the rising sun mark only the rays of the sun tend to look more like M's.

And speaking of fakes and reproductions let me warn you about the so-called "Nippon" dolls that are now being made. In my area they sell for around $10 and can be purchased from a lady who makes dolls and says she will gladly incise the word Nippon on the doll or doll head for a customer. They do look new but still they look a lot like the actual Nippon ones. Again let me stress, know your dealer and know your merchandise!

"Wildflower" (Reproduction)

Mocha set, pot is 11″ tall, set comes with four matching cups

Urn, 12″ tall

Large dresser jar, 7″ across

Egg box, 5⅜″ across

Tea strainer and receptacle, strainer is 5″ across

Footed box, 4⅞″ wide

Hinged powder box, 5¾″ across

Ewer

Trinket box, 5¾″ across

Dresser set, 5″ cologne bottle, 3½″ powder jar

Lidded sauce tureen, 7¾″ across

Green Mist (Reproduction)

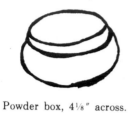

Sugar, 5½" across and creamer, 4" across.

Powder box, 4⅛" across.

Master sugar bowl, 6⅛" tall.

Crimped sugar bowl, 5½" across.

FAKE MARK

REAL MARK

FAKE MARK

REAL MARK

THE NORITAKE COMPANY

Nippon collectors owe a great debt to the Noritake Co. of Japan for most of the beautiful dishes they now own.

Correspondence I have had with the company confirms that 13 marks published in Series I of the Encyclopedia are backstamps of the Noritake Company or its predecessor, Morimura Bros.

Mark # 47, M in wreath was registered for the U.S. market in 1911

    # 52, maple leaf Nippon was first used by Morimura Bros. in 1891 and according to Noritake Co. records the green mark is indicative of "first grade" wares and the blue mark "second grade"

    # 66, Noritake M in wreath Nippon was registered in Japan in 1912

    # 68, Noritake/Nippon was made for export to the United States beginning in 1906

    # 80, RC Nippon was made for export to the United States beginning in 1906 and was registered for the U.S. market in 1911

    # 81, RC Noritake Nippon was made for export to the United States begining in 1906

    # 82, RC Noritake Nippon was made for the Japanese Market beginning in 1906

    # 88 & 89, Royal Kinran Nippon were made for the Japanese market, circa 1906

    # 91, Royal Nishiki was made for the Japanese market beginning in 1906

    # 92, Royal Satsuma Nippon was made for the Japanese Market beginning in 1906

    # 93, Royal Sometuke was also made for the Japanese market beginning in 1906

    #103, Spoke Nippon was made for export to the United States beginning in 1906

Studies show that these marks alone are found on more than 80% all the Nippon era dishes!

BACK STAMPS OF NORITAKE

The following information is provided by the Noritake Co.

(A)   MORIMURA BROTHERS ERA

    (1)   1878 - 1884

        There are records that during this period, Morimura Brothers had then their own decoration kiln in Japan, but what Back Stamp they used is unknown.

    (2)   1884 - 1890

        In 1882, Morimura Brothers changed their business nature to wholeselling from retailing, and they had dozens of their affiliated decoration factories all over Japan. Following are a few of the Back Stamps of that era.

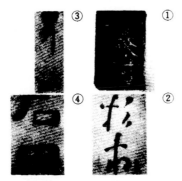

'Country of Origin' was marked in Chinese Characters, not in English. In 1890, 'The McKinley Tariff Act, was passed. The Declaration of the Country of Origin became necessary for all the products coming to U.S. since that time, 'Nippon' had appeared as part of Back Stamp until 'Japan' replaced it in 1921.

If it is painted in *Green Color* = 'First Grade' - If it is in *Blue Color* = '2nd Grade'

(3) 1891

(B) NORITAKE ERA

(4) 1904 - Noritake Factory was founded in 1904 in Noritake, a village in the vicinity of Nagoya, Aichi, Japan

(5) 1906 - (For Domestic Market in Japan)

Samples are not shown, but the following were for the Domestic Market in Japan

- Royal Satsuma   - Royal Someteke   - Royal Kinran
- Royal Kaita   - Royal Nishiki

(For Export To U.S.)

(6) 1908 - Registered in London -

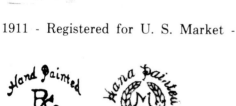

(7) 1911 - Registered for U. S. Market -

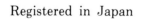

Registered in Japan

(8) 1912 -

(9) 1914 -

Applied for the first dinner set made in Noritake Factory.

Registered in India in 1926.

(10) 1921 -   (11) 1933 -

(12) 1946 - (After World War II)

(13) 1947 - Lasted only
       a year and half
(Should have been back
stamped "Rose China")

(14) 1949 -

(15)
1952 -
Current

12

HISTORY OF NORITAKE

The history of the Noritake Co., Limited (Nippon Toki Kabushiki Kaisha), Noritake, Nagoya, Japan was compiled in February, 1968 mainly for the important clients to the Noritake factory from foreign countries. The Noritake Co. has graciously consented to share this with readers of the Encyclopedia.

The history of Noritake begins with the history of Japan's export trade.

Founder of Noritake, Baron Ichizaemon Morimura was born in 1839 in a family of merchants who acted as purveyors to feudal lords. In 1859 when he was 20, the shogunate decided that a delegation be sent to the United States to return the courtesy visit of Commodore Perry in 1852 to Japanese shores. Baron Morimura was ordered to change Japanese money into American coin in the Yokohama foreign concession for the delegation to carry to the States. The Japanese money to be changed was gold of such high purity, while the currency to be received in exchange was coin of very low quality called Mexican silver. Feeling that it was a great loss to the country to allow gold of such high purity to flow out of Japan in this way, our founder, the late Baron I. Morimura spoke about the matter of Yukichi Fukuzawa, one of the great leaders in the modernization of new Japan from feudral shogunate-governing era. Fukuzawa told Morimura it was necessary to promote the export trade so that the gold coin that went out of Japan would flow back into the country.

Thus, Ichizaemon Morimura, young and ambitious Tokoyo boy founded Morimura Bros., Inc. at Ginza in Tokoyo in 1876 and started as trading firm in exporting traditional Japanese style of potteries, bamboo works and other Japanese curious gift items, so-called typical Japanese sundry goods to the United States, aiming at establishment of Japanese economy with export trade and branched out other retail and wholesale office in New York in 1877.

During its expansion of export business, Morimura Bros. decided to concentrate on ceramics, thus Noritake was founded by him in January 1, 1904 at the present site of main factory for the primary purpose of manufacturing and exporting high quality chinaware mainly to the United States; that means U.S.A. has been the greatest supporters and the biggest customers for Noritake since 1904.

The founders are Ichizaemon Morimura, Magobei Okura, Jitsuei Hirose, Yasukata Murai, Kazuchika Okura and Kotaro Asukai.

The technique to manufacture high quality dinnerware was mastered in 1910s and Noritake adopted streamlined mass-production system in 1920s and 1930s and enjoyed high reputation on the Noritake China all over the world.

In the course of the growth during that period, the Sanitary Ware Division of Noritake became independent from Noritake in 1917 which is named Toyo Toki Kaisha, Ltd. and known as the biggest sanitary ware and related metal fitting manufacturers in Japan.

Insulator Division of Noritake also became independent from Noritake in 1919, later splitting into two companies in 1936. One is known as NGK Insulator Co., Ltd., the world's biggest insulator manufacturers: the other is NGK Spark Plug Co., Ltd. (Nippon Tokushu Togyo Kaisha, Ltd.) which is the top manufacturers of spark plug in Japan and next to the American firm "Champion" in the world.

In 1939, Noritake which had been making extensive research on grinding wheels, decided to go into mass-production of bonded abrasive products in and after 1939 by utilizing long-experienced knowledge of ceramics. The high quality grinding wheels were in strong demand for Japanese industrial development and the many new products compiled with such demand in both its quality and its quantity.

Keeping steps with the rapid recovery and expansion of Japanese industries after World War 2nd, Noritake enlarged several times its production of grinding wheels by adding new kilns and modern equipments. Along with the technical improvement, Noritake added variety of wheels and related products to its production items to satisfy every particular needs in the industries and as a consequence has come to the position of the largest manufacturers of abrasive products such as grinding wheels, coated abrasives as well as grinding machines in Japan. Besides the main factory in Nagoya for Noritake China and vitrified abrasive products, Noritake now has Kamorai Plant completed in 1960 in the western suburb of Nagoya which manufactures Resinoid Wheels. It also has Coated Abrasive Factory in Miyoshi in the eastern suburb and Grinding Machine Factory in Komaki in the northern suburb.

Now, let's come back to the story of chinaware.

During the World War 2nd, the main chinaware factory here in Nagoya was seriously suffered from damage at equipment, resources of raw materials and employees who reduced to 1,000 from 4,000.

However, right after the War, the U.S. 8th Army and the Allied Occupation Forces, who quite well knew the fine quality of Noritake China, came in to Japan and set up Procurement Office to supply the needs for their Troop Housing Program as well as Dependent House Program.

To comply with this demand which was big enough to rehabilitate the factory, Noritake had resumed manufacturing chinaware with the warmhearted assistance of GHQ Industrial Division, Aichi Prefectural Military Government, QMC of Tokai Region and so forth who helped Noritake obtain the raw materials, fuels, liquid gold, packing materials etc. and also issued to Noritake huge blanket orders for financing and recovering purpose.

We can not forget their thoughtful consideration and kind arrangements of this nature, Noritake has rapidly recovered and increased the production and improved its quality.

In 1946 and 1947, however, Noritake did not like to supply to U.S. Military personnels under the brand name of "Noritake", but named it "Rose China" since Noritake could have no confidence to produce the high quality of pre-war standard deserved to the named "Noritake", due to shortage of superior raw materials, equipment and skillful employees. This was because Noritake did not like to spoil the high reputation of Noritake name established in the pre-war days in the United States. The U.S. Army Procurement Office kindly understood our situation and accepted our supply "Rose China" until 1948.

In 1947 Central Purchasing Office was established in Japan and started distributing Noritake China to Rycom, Philcom, Marbo and all other U.S. Exchanges in the Far East. Since then, we have been supplying Noritake China to U.S. Military PXs. In other word, PX has been the greatest supporters and the biggest patrons of Noritake in the past 20 years after the war.

During the course of resumption of foreign trade with U.S.A. and other country in and after 1948, Noritake has expanded extensively to become the largest chinaware manufacturers in the world and completed new Miyoshi Dinner Ware Plant in 1965 in the eastern end of Aichi Prefecture equipped with revolutionally modern mechanical processes.

Besides the chinaware plants, Noritake has now Stainless Flat Ware Factory in northern part of Central Japan, Atsugi Plant located near Tokyo which manufactures the high crystal glassware and also Melamineware Factory in Anjyo city near Nagoya which is also the biggest manufacturers of melamine table ware in Japan.

Now, among the monthly output of 5 million piece of chinaware, approx. 70% is exported to more than 90 countries and 70% out of the export goes to PX and the United States.

In the abrasives field Noritake had technical license agreement with Carbourundum Co. in U.S.A. and now become the biggest enterprise in Japan.

In its biggest market, United States Noritake Co., Inc. New York, which has now branches in Chicago, Los Angeles, Atlanta, Dallas, Seattle and Cincinnati was incorporated in 1948 to import and wholesale Noritake Products in the United States and Canada and now 30 staff from Noritake are stationed working with locally employed 70 personnels. The Foreign Trade Division of Noritake embraces 60 employees and the business to the world markets is increasing year by year. This is because Noritake has been manufacturing the best quality products to render full satisfaction to all of the dealers to prosper each other. Noritake will do moreover to serve the long-patronizing customer, U.S. Exchanges and other foreign customers.

Trade Names and Addresses in New York City, N.Y.

MORIMURA BROS. & CO.
MORIMURA BROS.
MORIMURA BROS., INC.

───────────○───────────────○───────────

1876	#97, Front Street	(Retailing)	(HINODE SHOKAI, formed in November)
1877	(HINODE SHOKAI, Fulton Street, (w/-Mr. M. Sato))		
1878	(HINODE SHOKAI, 238, 6th Avenue, (w/-Mr. M. Sato))		
1879	#238, 6th Avenue	(M.B. & CO.)	
1881	#221, 6th Avenue	(M.B. & CO.)	
1884	541, Broadway	(M. Bros.) (Wholesaler)	
1890	530, Broadway	(M. Bros.) (Wholesaler)	
1894	538, Broadway	(M. Bros.) (Wholesaler)	
1902	546, Broadway	(M. Bros.) (Wholesaler)	
1917	53-57, West 23rd Street	(M. Bros.) (Wholesaler)	
1921	53-57, West 23rd Street	(M.B. INC.)	
1941	Closed	(M.B. INC.)	
1976	Re-Opened	(M.B. INC.)	
	155, East 55th Street, New York City		

───

NORITAKE CO., INC

───────────○───────────────○───────────

1947	#125, East 23rd Street	
1951	212, 5th Avenue	(N. C. I)
1974	41, Madison Avenue	

NIPPON WAS PLENTIFUL IN THE EARLY
1900'S!

Our late 19th and early 20th century relatives were equally enamored with Nippon. A 1916 National Cloak and Suit Co., NYC catalog lists a pair of candlestick lamps for $1.75 a pair plus 5¢ for postage. A character bisque 5″ doll was $.35, a 6″ Kewpie doll was $.49 and a 5″ bisque Kewpie doll was $.25 plus 2¢ for postage. A page from a 1915 S&H catalog shows many different premiums that were available. Nippon dresser sets, ferners, chocolate sets, bowls, etc could be obtained from them. The Benner Tea Co. of Iowa was another that gave Japanese wares as premiums. They gave 10% of the purchase price in profit sharing coupons for these purchases.

An old Vantine catalog printed at the turn of the century gives us a clue to the varied pieces and prices available back then. A.A. Vantine & Co. was located at 77 & 79 Broadway, NYC and their catalogue "The Vantine Catalogue of Oriental Wares" has printed on the cover "a sort of guide book to the manifold and fascinating treasures of Japan, China, India, Turkey, Persia and the Holy Land, as imported by A.A. Vantine & Co.".

Over 150 styles of chocolate pots in floral figures and fanciful designs and beautiful colorings were offered. One could pick from 75 styles of Nippon cracker jars in all sizes from $.25 to $3.50. "Berry and ice cream sets consisting of one large dish and six saucers in a large assortment of shapes and decorations" could be purchased from $2.00 to $5.00 a set. "Teapots in all the well-known Japanese wares, as well as our own excellent designs, all sizes and shapes" vary from $.20 to $4.00 each.

One item was a tete-a-tete set which consisted of a teapot, sugar and creamer and two cups and saucers and was sold for $1.00 to $3.50 a set or the same set could be purchased with six cups and saucers for $3.00 to $6.00.

It's always interesting to find old catalogs and compare prices along with finding out the variety of patterns, sizes and shapes available back then. The catalog goes on to say "Japanese Table Porcelains. Few additions to the table service lend more beauty than the decorative yet serviceable porcelains from Japan. Their uniqueness makes them admirable for gift purposes!". And so it is today!

Many of the Nippon sets in demand:

Asparagus (painted and shaped like asparagus)
Berry
Bread and butter
Cake
Celery
Chocolate
Coaster
Coffee
Condiment
Corn (each shaped and painted like ears of corn)
Creamer and sugar
Demitasse or after dinner coffee set
Desk
Dinner
Dresser (also children's sizes)
Fish
Game
Ice cream (some have cups with silver holders)
Hostess
Lemonade
Liquor with pedestalled glasses
Luncheon
Mantle (often with a pair of candlesticks and vase or urn or two side vases)
Nut
Oatmeal (bowl, pitcher and plate)
Punch
Relish

Salad
Smoking
Snack plate and matching cup
Tankard and mugs or steins
Tea (including children's sizes)
Tete-a-tete (teapot, sugar, creamer, two cups and saucers)

Favorite scenes, designs and patterns collectors refer to, however, by no means inclusive as there are literally hundreds that could be collected.

Airplanes (circa WWI, monoplanes and biplanes)
Animals including the buffalo, camels, cows, deer, dogs, ducks, elephants, giraffes, horses, lions, moose, oxen, sheep, squirrels and tigers.
Arab scenes including the man on camel and woman at the Mosque
Art Deco
Art Nouveau
Beading and jeweling
Butterflies
Birds including blackbirds, bluebirds, cranes, flying geese, mythological hoo and griffin, mallard, owl, ostrich, pelican, pheasant, stork, swallow and swans.

Cars
Castles
Cloisonné
Cobalt with gold
Cobalt with swans
Coralene
Cottages
Decalcomanias
Desert ruins
Diaper patterns
Doll face
Dragon
Dutch people
English coach
Egyptian Nile scene with war ship
Egyptian palm scene
Egyptian lady
Farm scenes
Fish still life pictures
Fishing scenes with fisherman
Flowers
Fruit still life pictures
Geisha girl
Geometrics
Gold on white
Gold overlay
Gold with turquoise beading

Gouda
Halloween scene
Incised decoration
Indian
Knights in armor
Macabre designs including the devil, skull, etc.
Monks
Moriage
Nuts, including peanuts, chestnuts and acorns
Pirates
Portraits
Roman chariots
Sailboat scenes
Silhouettes
Silver overlay
Snow scenes
Sometsuke
Sprigged-on decoration
Stamped decor
Souvenir
Tapestry
Transfers
Tree scenes
Wedgwood
Willow pattern
Windmills
Woodland scene

NIPPON POTPOURRI AND OTHER INTERESTING FACTS

Summer months are a good time to collect rose petals for filling your Nippon rose or potpourri jar. Of course, roses received anytime during the year can also be used.

The potpourri jar was usually made with two covers. The top cover is often domed and has pierced holes. Under this cover is another cover, only solid and when removed allowed the aroma of the potpourri mixture to permeate through the house.

To make a rose mixture it's necessary to gather roses in the morning after the dew has evaporated. When using those from a bouquet wait till the roses have peaked but before the petals turn brown. Discard the stems and leaves and lay on paper toweling and dry for three to four days out of sunlight.

Once dried it's necessary to add some spices. In a large mixing bowl combine with a spoon 5 cups of petals, ½ tsp. cinnamon, ½ tsp. nutmeg, ½ tsp. cloves (also mace and/or allspice if desired). A fixative should be added to preserve the scent, either one oz. of oris root or 1 tablespoon of dried lavender or oak moss which are available at most herb shops and drugstores.

Transfer the mixture to a covered jar and store for several weeks. Shake occasionally. Newly dried petals may be added from time to time, also two to three drops of a favorite perfume. For extra aroma add a cinnamon stick or the peel of one lemon, grated and dried.

For a potpourri mixture add other dried blossoms to the rose petals such as jasmine, pinks, lavenders and carnations. Even bits of dried orange peels and leaves of pungent herbs add a nice touch.

After three to four weeks scoop some of the mixture into your potpourri or rose jar and enjoy nature's own room freshener.

Rose bowls were also used years ago. These are generally 4-6″ in diameter and many are found with ruffled or pinched edges. Dried rose petals were placed in them, hence the name rose bowl.

Cinnamon stick holders were another favorite. The top on these however is generally flat and they have much larger openings than the potpourri jar. Cinnamon sticks were placed in the holes and made for a pleasant "cover-up" of household odors.

Our Nippon collectibles reflect the past manners and customs of our ancestors and are our link with the bye-gone days. Many times we see some of these unusual items only to wonder what they were used for.

Years ago a "nest" of egg cups could be found at the breakfast table. There are both single and double egg cups. The double one is larger in size and is actually two cups in one. The larger cup seems to be mounted atop the smaller one. Some single cups are even found with an attached plate which could have been used for pieces of the egg shell. (See plate #'s 284, 285, 696 & 1179)

Egg warmers usually have space for four to six eggs. They also have a handle and a porcelain stopper in the middle. The stopper can be removed and warm water placed in the unit. The stopper is then replaced and this kept the eggs warm for a period of time. Don't be fooled if you find one of these with a cork for a stopper. They were originally manufactured with a porcelain stopper not a cork one. (See plate #'s 582 & 1178)

Then there are egg servers used on the table naturally to serve eggs. These are found with egg shaped indentations and come in several styles and sizes. (See plate # 1180)

Porcelain blotter corners were often part of a desk set and came in sets of four. Many were broken and sometimes we only find one, two or possibly three remaining. I have seen these advertised from everything from a wall pocket to a hand held ashtray. Be informed, know what you're buying and selling. (See plate # 835)

Invalid feeders (also called feeding boats or pap boats) are handled cups with long spouts. They were used to put food in the mouth of those unable to feed themselves, such as someone confined to bed or a person with broken arms, etc. Broth and cereal were usually used in the feeder. (See plate # 1172)

Pancake servers are two piece items and have domed covers. The covers generally have two steam holes making the top vented.

The butter dish is a three piece item including the base piece, cover and porcelain insert. Ice was placed in the bottom piece then the insert was placed on top. Butter was put on top of the insert and this helped to keep it chilled. A butter tub serves the same purpose but has no cover and the bottom piece is usually handled and high walled. This has a similar perforated disc to separate the ice and the butter.

Tea strainers are two piece items which consist of the strainer and bottom receptacle. Loose tea was used years ago, not tea bags and often times tea would get in the cup. In order to avoid this the tea strainer was placed over the cup and the tea poured through it. Most of the loose tea was caught in the strainer and then the strainer was placed back on the base piece to drip. Due to the advent of the tea bag this is not an item readily needed today. (See plate #'s 287, 1183 & 1184)

Many people get confused as to the difference between an individual teapot and a syrup container. Both are about the same size but the clue to deciding which is which is that the teapot has a steam hole in the cover. This was not necessary on the syrup.

To better understand the Japanese culture it's necessary to know something of their tea ceremony, cha-no-yu, which literally means "hot water for tea". The tea plant is a native of Southern China and originated as a medicine before it became a popular beverage in both countries.

Ancient Japanese tea masters had a love of simplicity and the ceremony was conducted on a modest scale avoiding anything showy. According to Seno Tanaka, author of "The Tea Ceremony", "etiquette, spirituality and knowledge are necessary elements for the understanding of the tea ceremony".

The Japanese tea room was indicative of simplicity and purism. Ancient ones were empty except for some special object brought in for the occasion. In fact, Rikyu (a famous tea master) believed that flowers at the ceremony should be arranged as you would find them in a field.

Guests entered one by one noiselessly and took their seats. The host entered after all the guests were seated. Originally the tea service began as a worship of tea and a reverent mood still prevails today.

As the popularity of the tea ceremony increased new kilns sprang up all over Japan and they originally led to the making of a type of pottery called raku yaki.

There is a noticeable absence of symmetry in "true" Japanese art objects as repetition was considered fatal to the freshness of imagination.

Listed below are some of the Japanese terms associated with the tea ceremony:

cha bana... tea box for all tea utensils

cha do... tea teachings

cha-e... early name for the tea ceremony

cha ire... tea jars

cha jin... tea master (tea men)

cha ki... pottery utensils (tea things)

cha no yu... tea ceremony or hot water for tea

cha shitsu... tea room

cha wan... tea cups

JAPANESE SYMBOLS, CRESTS AND MONS

Symbols and crests are used on many of the Japanese wares in the design and sometimes as part of the backstamp.

Birds are important to the Japanese and it's customary for certain birds to be depicted with specific trees, for example: the pine with cranes and the bamboo with sparrows. Other symbols found together are the peony and peacock and the crane and the tortoise. Birds and animals looking up at the sky indicate to the Japanese ease and peace of mind.

Our wake up symbol, the rooster, is also a sign for rising early in the morning in Japan. Roosters are sacred and considered to be a sign of industriousness.

Other symbols found are the elephant which stands for wisdom and the cat which is viewed as both good and bad luck. The maple leaf means good luck. The peach tree stands for long life and a happy marriage while peach blossoms stand for feminine qualities, peacefulness and softness.

Lobsters, shrimp and prawn (considered the old of the sea) are symbols of long life and the bat is a harbinger of good fortune.

Japan's culture is related to nature and simplicity and gaudy decoration was contrary to Japanese taste. During the heyday of the "Nippon" era though many pieces were decorated merely to suit the Western market.

The followng ten Japanese crests are printed with the permission of Ernest Lehner, author of "Symbols, Signs and Signets" published by Dover Publications, Inc. in 1969.

#840 bamboo
#900 crane
#901 dove
#902 tortoise
#903 phoenix
#904 lobster
#905 crab
#908 lions
#909 horse
#910 hare

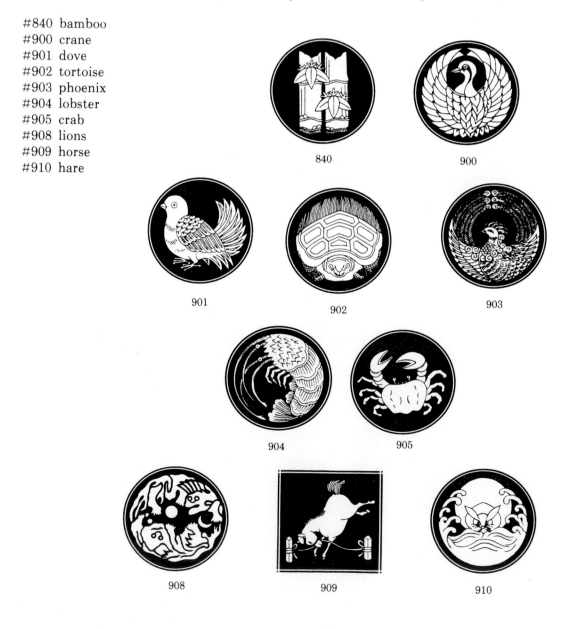

840   900

901   902   903

904   905

908   909   910

NIPPON CORALENE

Nippon marked coralene pieces are unusual to find but do exist. The mark is a semi circle rising sun above the words RS NIPPON. Most Japanese coralene items, however, are stamped "Patented 2/9/1909 Japan 912171", others are marked "Patent Applied For No. 38257 with Japanese markings included", "Kinran Patent N. 16137 Japan", or the RS mark is often found backstamped on items with the word Japan instead of Nippon appearing.

There is a wide variety of pieces to be found, vases, ferners, lamps, ewers, teapots, etc. and in an assortment of designs, florals, scenics, geometrics, even birds and dragons to mention a few. Most backgrounds have a matte finish.

Collectors should be careful to check the items for missing beads and it is advisable to not soak the pieces in water when cleaning as the beading may fall off.

A.L. Rock, an American living in Yokohama, Japan was the first to perfect this technique and apply for a patent.

There has been a lot of confusion as to what constitutes coralene beading and how it was manufactured and in an attempt to clean up any misconceptions regarding these pieces a copy of the original patent has been secured and is included for reference.

A. L. ROCK.
POTTERY ORNAMENTATION
APPLICATION FILED AUG. 19, 1908.

912,171.

Patented Feb. 9, 1909.

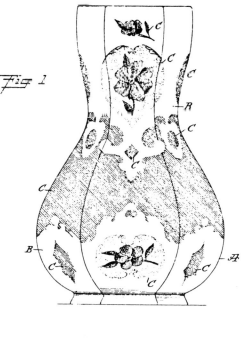

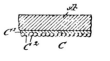

WITNESSES

INVENTOR
Alban L. Rock
BY
ATTORNEYS

UNITED STATES PATENT OFFICE.

ALBAN L. ROCK, OF YOKOHAMA, JAPAN, ASSIGNOR TO A. A. VANTINE & CO., OF NEW YORK, N. Y., A CORPORATION OF NEW JERSEY.

POTTERY ORNAMENTATION.

No. 912,171.   Specification of Letters Patent.   Patented Feb 9, 1909

Application filed August 19, 1908. Serial No. 449,223.

To all whom it may concern;

Be it known, that I, ALBAN L. ROCK, a citizen of the United States, at present residing in Yokohama, Japan, have invented
5 a new and Improved Pottery Ornamentation, of which the following is a full, clear, and exact description.

The object of the invention is to provide a new and improved pottery ornamentation, the
10 ornamentation being arranged to produce a permanent glass bead effect on porcelain vases and other pottery articles, in such a manner that the colorless transparent glass beads are fused in position on the body of the
15 pottery article by a fusing pigment which produces color effect in any predetermined design.

The invention consists of novel features and parts and combinations of the same, which
20 will be more fully described herein-after and then pointed out in the claim.

A practical embodiment of the invention is represented in the accompanying drawings, forming a part of this specification, in which
25 similar characters of reference indicate corresponding parts in all the views.

Figure 1 is a side elevation of a vase showing the improvement and produced according to my method; Fig. 2 is an enlarged side
30 elevation of part of the same; and Fig. 3 is a transverse section of the same.

A portion of the surface of the body A of the base shown in Fig. 1, is ornamented by a suitable gold ornamentation B, and the
35 remaining surface portion is covered by a glass bead ornamentation C, which consists of a fusing and carrying medium C' and colorless transparent glass beads C² fused to the surface of the body A by the said fusing and carrying
40 medium C'. The beads C² are comparatively small and are preferably spherical in shape, and the fusing and carrying medium C' maybe in a plain uniform color or in many colors, according to predetermined design, as
45 indicated at the portions representing the flowers on the vase shown in Fig. 1. The fusing and carrying medium C' consists of porcelain pigments and a fusible matter, either mixed together prior to the application on the body,
50 or applying the said pigments first and then the fusible matter. Sometimes both methods are used on the same article. As a rule, color work on porcelain showing bead decorations,
55 is done in a dull color effect by means of mixing shiroye, balsam copaiba with oil of turpentine, and then the outline of the bead design is done by a specially prepared pigment which when fired results in the gold-moriage.
60 The principal components of the fusible matter are 248 grains of silicate of albumen (shiroye) and 192 grains of flux (hakukyoku) to which is added as a carrying medium about
65 9.6 grains of a dry procelain pigment or color, the several ingredients being mixed with a certain percentage of water and all parts are well ground together. The porcelain color or pigment used with the fusible matter to form the fusible and carrying medium C' must be
70 of such a shade as can be fired satisfactorily at a uniform degree of heat, as otherwise some of the colors will not be fired enough while other shades may be fired too much, and the
75 slightest mistake in the selection of color shades in this respect tends to spoil the article.

In practice, the fusing and carrying medium C' is applied to the body of the vase in a wet
80 state, and then the colorless transparent glass beads C² are placed onto the said wet fusing and carrying medium, which holds the beads in position one alongside the other, as the rear portions of the beads are pressed into the wet
95 medium. The vase or other article thus decorated is then fired in the usual manner, so that the beads are fused with their rear portions onto the porcelain body by the fusing and carrying medium, to permanently fix the
90 beads in place without destroying their brilliant effect, enhanced by the underlying color pigment arranged accordingly to a predetermined design representing flowers
95 and other objects.

It is understood that the colors of the fusing and carrying medium are refracted through the glass beads, thus giving the vase a very fine appearance in a plush effect.
100

It is understood that the selection of the fusible and carrying medium and the degree of heat used in firing is of importance as the fusible matter must necessarily fuse at a lower
105 degree than the glass beads C², so that only the rear portions of the glass beads which are in contact with the fusible matter melt and fuse with the fusible matter, fused and adhering to the body A of the vase or like
110 article.

It is important in the use of the glass bead covering for the predetermined pattern for the different particles to lie closely together and to be distributed thus uniformly in close contact with each other throughout the area of the pattern produced upon the vase or other article and this is accomplished by the form of beads and the fusing of said beads upon the pattern as distinguished from the production of a granulated surface which might vary both as to size and proximity of its particles. The glass granulated material is produced directly upon a pane of glass or the like. By the beaded construction it will be noticed that the surface ornamentation of the vase or other article will be approximately smooth and simulate a plain surface as to touch without affecting the beauty of appearance gained by the spherical form of the beads as shown.

Having thus described my invention, I claim as new and desire to secure by Letters Patent:

A vase or like pottery article having a body, a fusing and carrying medium disposed on said body and colored and shaped to conform to a predetermined design, and comparatively small colorless spherical transparent beads arranged in contact with each other and covering the carrying medium and fused into connection therewith and following the outline of the design produced by the fusing and carrying medium, whereby to form a covering for the medium which will be uniform throughout the extent of the design and through which the said medium will be refracted, giving to the article an ornamented appearance in plush effect.

In testimony whereof I have signed my name to this specification in the presence of two subscribing witnesses.

ALBAN L. ROCK.

Witness:
Genji Kuribara,
Masataro O. Kasava.

ADVERTIQUES

Charles Whittier once wrote "Advertising succeeds according to the number of people it influences to take action. There is no other measure of its effectiveness. If it doesn't make people buy something or do something, the advertising is a failure."

Advertising items are as popular today as they were in the Nippon era. These pieces are usually given away or sold for a very nominal cost. They're intended to advertise a particular product or company and increase sales.

The majority of Nippon advertiques were made cheaply and have not survived over the years. Businesses often had their message printed on the item. Because so many of them were given away we often find the quality of porcelain somewhat lacking.

One popular item is the combination matchbox holder and ashtray which advertised Fatima Turkish Blend Cigarettes from the Liggett and Myers Tobacco Co. These pieces are decal trimmed featuring a veiled Turkish woman along with a red Maltese cross and the star and crescent. These items are not uniquely "Nippon" as a check with two different Roseville Pottery books indicate that this item was also manufactured by the Roseville Co. but most likely before 1916.

Checking with a collector of cigarette related items this information was obtained: "I also have the same ashtray but on the back it is marked made in Austria for J.R. Gibney.

From information, I have, I would say that the earliest this could be is 1912. When the tobacco trust (the original American Tobacco Co.) was broken in late 1911 the Fatima brand was given to Liggett & Myers Tobacco Co.

I would think this is a give away item. I do not recall seeing this item in any of the premium catalogs by Liggett & Myers during the approximate time period the ashtray was issued. The fact that it was issued from Austria would indicate that it was prior to World War II or at least before the U.S. entered the war. The Fatima brand is still made by Liggett & Myers today (without the successor to Cameron and Cameron added.)

The "Nippon" Fatima matchbox/ashtray has printed on it "Fatima Turkish Blend Cigarettes, Cameron & Cameron Co., Richmond, Va., Liggett & Myers Tobacco Co., Successor, No Gold Tips, Finest Quality". This item is backstamped with a green under the glaze mark saying NIPPON D13495.

Another unusual Nippon item to be found is the Ogilvie porcelain rolling pin which was once sold as a $.50 premium and had "We Use Royal Household Flour, Canada's Best Flour" printed on it.

China rolling pins became very popular in the late 19th and early 20th century and anyone lucky enough to have one of the originals made during the WWI period has quite a find.

"DOLL"ING UP YOUR HOUSE WITH NIPPON

The dictionary describes a doll as a child's toy baby but collecting dolls is hardly child's play to the serious collector. Dolls have been with us for thousands of years and they are mankind's oldest playthings. History books tell us that ancient ones were used as idols and in religious ceremonies, many were buried with the dead and most were not used as toys as we know them.

Dolls tend to remind us of our childhood and today there is a growing legion of doll collectors. It can, however, be a very expensive hobby to enter into although the majority of Nippon marked ones are still within the reach of most collector's pocketbooks.

Japan is a country noted for producing beautiful ceremonial dolls. In fact, the third of March each year is designated as Dolls' Festival and has been known to exist for over 900 years. It is a time when little girls set up displays of their dolls, many of which are heirlooms, having been passed down from generation to generation. The Japanese believe that these dolls reflect Oriental life and traditions. This occasion honors the daughters of the family while two months later a similar festival is held in May (5th) which is called Children's Day (originally Boys' Day). These doll festivals are occasions where friends and relatives gather to view the displays and enjoy refreshments.

Girls' Day (also known as the Peach Festival) is called Hina Matsuri in Japanese.

Several days before the Festival begins the house is thoroughly cleaned and the dolls are taken from their boxes where they have been safely stored all year. The dolls which usually number 15 are placed in the best room of the house. They are then arranged in a special order on steps which have been covered with a red cloth. The dolls' stand is a tier of shelves or steps and called hina-dan. The top shelf has miniature folding screens. In front of these screens are placed dolls representing the Emperor and Empress dressed in ancient costumes. The second step becomes the garden steps of the palace of Kyoto. This step and the remaining ones have the court attendants, ministers, ladies in waiting, court musicans and dancers. Miniature furniture and trees are also placed on the shelves. The bottom shelves contain decorative miniatures. Peach blossoms are arranged carefully around the dolls. These flowers represent happiness in marriage and also stand for feminine qualities, peacefulness, softness and mildness.

The young girls in the family are encouraged to invite their friends and relatives to enjoy the display and refreshments during the three day ceremony. The girls are responsible for planning the menu and shopping. Tiny fish, small vegetables and cakes and tea are served.

Japanese store windows are also decorated with peach and cherry blossoms at this time.

The fifth of May is set aside as a special holiday when displays of figures of Japanese heroes and warriors abound. This is called Children's Day (originally Boys' Day) and referred to as Kodomoul-Hi in Japanese. Colored banners made of cloth or paper in the shape of brightly colored fish are flown on this day in front of houses where boys live. Carp shaped flags are flown because the carp is symbolic of strength.

The boys' display usually consists of 3-4 steps covered with a green cloth. The top shelf has banners showing drawings of famous battles. Placed on the steps are dolls which represent Samurai warriors and dolls in ancient dress. Horses are also included. Vases of iris flowers are used in the display as the iris is sword-like and the Japanese associate them with warriors. The dolls are given to boys for display and are not used as toys. They are put away after the festival and stored until the next year. Refreshments are also served at this occasion.

Dolls from both festivals are considered "family heirlooms". It is thought that since these dolls have received the love of many generations they have also acquired souls and are treated accordingly.

Dolls have appealed to the Japanese for ages, however, most of the dolls backstamped Nippon which were exported to the United States were merely copies of European versions and not Japanese dolls in the traditional sense. The Japanese flagrantly ignored US and European copyrights and imitated all the popular dolls of that time period. All types were copied, whatever the West wanted the Japanese happily and capably supplied. There seem to be Nippon dolls to please everyone, from the neophyte to the advanced collector and both Nippon and doll collectors are beginning to buy up all that are available.

The actual heyday of producing most of the children's items began during World War I when doll manufacturing in Germany was brought to a halt. Japan took over the lead in this field and soon glutted the market with dolls and toys to delight little people everywhere.

For years, Nippon marked dolls and toys have been ignored by collectors, most likely because the quality was not as good as that found on many European counterparts. It must be noted that these items are not works of art but then we must remember that they were never intended to be. They were mass produced, sold cheaply and meant to be played with. Many were broken or thrown away, actually it's amazing that so many have survived all these years. Because of this, there are only a limited number to be found and diligent searching on the part of the collector is often required.

Nippon toys may be small in size but now collectors will find that the price tag is just the reverse. These collectibles have been "sleepers" that are now awakening with a loud cry!

Some of the dolls are all-bisque, while others have cloth, composition or kid bodies. They range in size from the tiny ones which were used for play in dollhouses to the larger ones that have eyes that open and close. Others have molded clothes, some have their clothes painted on. Many have wigs, some are even jointed. There were even small dolls made specifically to decorate birthday and wedding cakes. Collectors will discover that Nippon boy dolls are harder to find (evidently they were not as popular with little girls of long ago) and their scarcity seems to be reflected in their price.

Many of the small all-bisque dolls were sold with crepe paper clothing and every now and then one can still be found in its original condition. Most collectors will find that the bisque jointed arms on the small dolls are usually of poorer quality than the rest of the body. Many have become broken over the years and replaced, usually with a better quality reproduction than the original piece and this can often be a clue to the collector if the arms are original.

The marks are usually found incised on the back of the doll, sometimes on the doll's shoulders or head, other times it can be found on the bottom of the feet. Some originally came with labels or stickers but many of these have since worn off or been removed.

Old mail order catalogs advertised separate doll heads and bodies for sale so if one part became broken a new one could be purchased. Some of the known companies that once distributed Nippon dolls are Son Brothers, San Francisco; Taiyo Trading Co., NYC and Toronto; Louis Wolf and Co., Boston and NYC; Fould and Freure, NYC; and Morimura Bros., NYC.

One of the unique small dolls is Queue San Baby which was distributed by Morimura Bros. This doll can be found in both a standing or kneeling position and has molded slippers, molded cap on its head and a queue (long braid) down its back. It originally came with a sticker on its chest giving its name. Both boy and girl Queue San Babies can be found.

There is also the Polynesian doll dressed in a straw skirt, sure to please the collector. Or how about the doll found sitting in her own bathtub. There are also the Nippon imitations of Happifats which were copies of those made by the Borgfeldt Co. from the drawings of Kate Jordan. These little dolls have rotund bodies and molded suits and dresses. Copies of Rose O'Neill's famous elflike creatures, Kewpies, can also be found. They have darling faces and little blue wings. Their arms are usually extended, they have little molded tufts of hair and make a nice addition to any collection. Baby Bud is another favorite and is usually found with his name incised on the back of his shoulders. Baby Darling has a molded ribbon in her hair and some can still be found bearing the Baby Darling sticker. Others, collectors are fond of are the Dolly doll, World War I pilots, soldiers and medics, Dutch children and even Little Red Riding Hood.

Collectors categorize dolls into (1) baby dolls, (2) small child dolls and (3) older person dolls. Some are character dolls and represent famous people or fictional characters. Collectors will also find pincushion or half-dolls which usually have a molded hat or hair. Most Nippon ones are found highly glazed and dressed in elaborate dresses and costumes. Some have fancy wide brimmed hats, others pompadour hair styles with the hair brushed straight back from the forehead. Some will even have hair that has often been painted with comb marks. A number hold items such as fans, mirrors and animals.

The half-dolls were often sold in dime stores and some were made into pincushion dolls, while some adorned lamp shades, others were made into telephone covers or dresser ornaments. Many have sew holes in the base rim while still others had corks or stoppers as tops for bottles. A number were used to decorate cakes and some will be found having a cloth skirt which originally covered a tea pot (tea cozy).

The small all-bisque dolls are often referred to as "candy store" or "penny dolls" because their original owners usually purchased them in the neighborhood dime or candy store. In searching old catalogs we find that typical prices in 1918 for 4½" bisque dolls were $.42 a dozen, that's less than $.04 each!

Collectors will find that different dolls vary according to the clay used, the firing process employed and the artist's skill when painting the features, etc.

The different bodies shown in this book are either bisque, composition, kid or cloth. The composition bodies have a hard finish, almost unbreakable, however, they do tend to craze and crack. A number of combinations were originally used, some were basically a glue and flour mixture, others resin, wood pulp, sawdust, starch and water. All were molded and then baked to obtain the desired finish and most have a "varnished" appearance.

The intention of this book is not to cover every doll produced nor each process used in their manufacture. It is meant merely as a guide to some of the dolls available and to possibly whet the appetite for further purchases. Several good books are devoted exclusively to dolls and many are listed in the bibliography. A number of them go into considerable detail and will undoubtedly be of help to the advanced as well as the beginning collector.

Many of the dolls shown in this Encyclopedia are all-bisque or half-bisque. Both terms are pretty much self descriptive. These dolls were made of clay which has been molded and fired at very high temperatures. All dolls shrink in size in both the drying of the greenware and during the firing. They were then sanded down, painted and refired. Some dolls required several firings. Bisque dolls have a dull (non-reflective) look. Their appearance is a non-glossy finish and their coloring is permanent.

A so-called "china" finish on a doll is one where the doll has been molded, fired and been highly glazed. It has a shiny, almost glasslike appearance. Many of the pincushion dolls are found with this "china" finish.

Some dolls will be found that have ears that have been molded separately then applied to the head. Some even have nostril openings and are referred to by collectors as breathers.

The choice of what to collect is endless, whatever seems to strike the collector's fancy. Those who collect dolls know that "it's the little things in life that count" for their dolls provide them with a constant source of pleasure. The original owners may long have outgrown these toys but the collector certainly has not!

W. H. Davies once wrote "If life is to made interesting and worth its breath, we must look on ourselves as growing children right up to the end of our days." Such is the wonderful experience that awaits the collector of dolls for it truly is a "small" world after all.

HELPFUL HINTS ON HOW TO CARE FOR YOUR NIPPON DOLLS

Probably the best advice to collectors would be to use old fashioned common sense in the care of their items. Dolls should be kept at room temperature at all times. They should not be subjected to drastic changes in temperature such as storing them in attics or garages. Humid cellars are also dangerous due to the possibility of mildew and mold. They should be kept out of direct sunlight and placed in an area where it is not too dry or too humid. Composition dolls are subject to cracking and crazing so one has to be extra careful with the care of them.

If you do not have room to display all the dolls and need to store them it is advisable to follow some basic rules. A doll with sleeping eyes should always be placed face down. Dolls with jointed china or bisque legs need to have a spacer placed between the feet so they do not hit against each other. A large wooden bead or spool will work nicely.

Drawers and cedar chests make good storage places. If you don't wrap the dolls with paper at least store them so they can't touch each other. Put dividers between them, foam rubber, cardboard, etc. If you decide to wrap them use a sufficient amount of white tissue to cover the doll and then wrap with newspaper. Never just wrap in newspaper alone as the newsprint can rub off on the doll. Newspaper, however, makes good liners for drawers and cabinets as it helps ward off insects. Also be sure to use moth balls or crystals, etc. to prevent bugs from destroying the cloth, kid or composition bodies.

When cleaning all bisque or bisque head dolls use a mild soap and warm water to get them clean. Work very gently with a soft cloth. I have also found that a soft toothbrush or Q-tip is good to use for those hard to reach places.

It's always exciting to find dolls in their original clothes but we have to remember that most of these dolls are 60-70 years old and the majority have had many changes of clothing over the years. I try to keep my dolls in the clothes they were wearing when I purchased them, however, if you do wish to change them, doll experts advise that you put away the original set of clothing and label it. Someday a new owner may delight in having these items.

Try to buy the best possible in the beginning. If the doll is valuable and needs repairing take it to a professional restorer. Some jobs can easily be done by the collector such as restringing arms and legs but others are just beyond most collectors' ability.

As with all valuable items keep them out of the way of small children and family pets. Don't leave them out where they can get knocked over and broken.

Buy the best you can initially. Always try to buy items free of cracks, hairlines, chips, etc. But most of all, buy what *you* like! Ladies' fashions go in cycles, so too antiques and collectibles. What is popular today may not be a decade from now.

CHILDREN'S TOY CHINAWARE, FEEDING DISHES & NOVELTIES

The difference between collectors and children is often the price of their toys! And so it is today with the small Nippon collectibles that were once used by small children. It is difficult to locate an entire tea set in perfect condition because they were played with. Usually a plate may be chipped, a piece missing, handles broken and finials, etc. Lucky is the collector who finds all the pieces in "mint" condition.

Today we are able to find the play dishes in a variety of patterns, some have pictures of children on them, others have animals, silhouettes, nursery characters, etc., anything that appealed to the small child. There were children's sets for use when little girls had their friends in for tea, dolls' dishes for doll tea parties and smallest of all, the dollhouse dishes.

Whatever mother had, daughter was able to acquire a smaller replica. In fact, some of the old catalog ads for these dishes tell us that the items are almost like mother's in both size and quality. "This set would delight any little girl. Made of very fine thin white china, beautifully decorated in enameled picture designs taken from fairy tales; with gold traced edges and handles relieved with floral decorations on the larger pieces. This is a very large size, for practical use, and will be very highly appreciated by the children."

One of the favorite patterns of those who collect children's items is the "doll face" (also referred to at times as child's face or boy's face). This pattern does vary on certain pieces but basically the dishes were manufactured in the same manner and resemble each other. In this style we can find a cereal bowl, mug, plate, creamer, hanging plaque, egg cup, salt and pepper set, cup, almost everything imaginable that would appeal to a child. These items have a marked resemblance to the Campbell Kids and again it is possible that the Japanese copied this delightful pair. The Campbell Soup Co., however, is unable to identify any of these pieces as being licensed consumer premiums of the Kids offered at any time by Campbells.

They did provide the following information however, "The Campbell Kids were created by the artist, Grace Wiederseim, later known as Grace Gebbie Drayton, in 1900. The Kids never had first names—no ear or necks ever show. Most people think that the Kids are twins, but they're not. They were first used on car cards in Philadelphia streetcars."

Grace Drayton originated and illustrated the Bobby Blake and Dolly Drake comic series for the *Philadelphia Press* and the *Evening Journal* among others. All Grace Drayton's characters looked similar, they had fat tummies, round faces, fat cheeks, they were pleasant little plump children often referred to as Drayton characters. Many readers of her comic strips automaticaly started calling the Kids Dolly and Bobby because of their similarity to the Kids but the Campbell Co. has never officially named them. The Japanese also named the children's tea set in the doll face pattern the "Dolly" tea set. It could have been named after Grace Drayton's characters or else it might just been a reference to it being for the doll.

As early as 1910 doll makers capitalized on the popularity of The Kids and soon other doll makers, smelling success in Grace's "babies", reproduced them in great quantites.

The Nippon doll face items are known to date back as far as 1915 but probably could have been manufactured as early as 1910.

The Campbell Kids are among the most widely featured and lovable characters in the history of American advertising and they could be a link to the Nippon doll face pieces.

Some of the other sets were decorated with scenes of children playing or nursery rhyme characters. Happifats and the Sunbonnet Babies can also be found.

The Sunbonnet Babies were originally illustrated in the early 1900's by Bertha Corbett in the Sunbonnet Primer. Their faces were always hidden by sunbonnets and they were depicted in various scenes, baking, sweeping, scrubbing, reading, knitting, mending, ironing, washday and fishing.

Happifats was not only a popular Nippon doll but this design can also be found on tea sets and miniature dresser sets consisting of a hatpin holder, hair receiver, powder box, all on an oval dresser tray.

Children's feeding dishes also come in many patterns and sizes. There were mug and bowl sets, dishes with compartments, cups, creamers, etc. Many of the dishes were thick rimmed with wide or weighted bottoms.

Then there are the other collectible children's pieces. Even nightlights were manufactured, some were molded in the shape of a bunny, owl and also a little Dutch girl. These were two piece items, the top lifted off and a candle was placed inside. A hole in the top let the light shine through. Some are found that have even been electrified. What an adorable accessory this must have been for a child's room.

Big collectors like small collectibles and many search for the figural items which include a ballerina, an Indian maiden, dogs, birds, alligators and even miniature Dutch shoes. Popular comic characters also had items fashioned after them and today we can find Jiggs of the "Bringing Up Father" series depicted on several items.

RCA's beloved Little Nipper is probably the most recognized dog in the world and is the main figure in the logo of the RCA Corp. trademark "His Master's Voice". He is now more than 80 years old and has appeared on millions of records, phonographs, advertisements, etc. over the years.

Due to the enthusiams of collectors Nipper is now enjoying a resurgence in popularity. As with everything else the Japanese knew a good thing when they saw it and soon were manufacturing Nippon Nipper novelty items identical to those made in Germany. On the bottom of each is stamped, under the glaze, "Hand Painted Nippon" or "Nippon" plus a number written in bright gold paint. To date four different #'s have been brought to my attention but I am sure there are many more to be found. All are souvenir pieces, one says "Souvenir of Colorado Springs, Colo." and has #247 on it. Another says "Souvenir of New London, Conn." with #20 and the other two are marked "Souvenir of Burlington, Vt." along with the #221 and "Souvenir of Watertown", #35. So far these numbers pose a mystery as to their meaning.

The items are small in size but unfortunately for most collectors are sizeable in price. They measure 3″ high and the base is 4½″ long.

One was seen at a show recently that was identical to the Nippon piece only marked Germany as country of manufacture. It was in sad shape though, the city's name even worn off and still priced at a hefty $225.

Evidently the Nippon marked ones were made during the WWI period and probably between the years of 1916-1921 when the United States stopped importing items from Germany.

In an effort to learn more about these items I wrote directly to the RCA Corp. in Indianapolis, Indiana. I received the following information.

"Little Nipper was a real fox terrier owned originally by the brother of an English artist. When the dog's owner died, the little animal became the pet of the artist.

One day in the late 1800's the artist, Francis Barraud, discovered the dog listening to an old-style horn-speaker phonograph with head cocked. The artist concluded the terrier thought he was hearing his original master's voice. Hence the painting and the title "His Master's Voice".

The painting became the property of the Victor Talking Machine Company in 1901 and the artist was permitted to paint a number of "originals" to supplement the annual royalty paid him by Victor to use the painting in various promotions.

When the Victor Company was acquired by RCA in 1929, the picture became the property of RCA and was used for years as the company's trademark. Some ten years ago, the trademark with the fox terrier was phased out in view of the company's growing status as a worldwide corporate entity. However, Little Nipper has been revived as part of the RCA logotype and is widely used today.

We are however, unable to confirm any data on the dissemination of Nipper novelty pieces."

So it turns out that our all-American symbol was not even homegrown after all but "imported" to our shores. It was painted by an English artist and the novelty pieces were manufactured in both Germany and Japan.

Facsimiles of marks found on Nippon items

BABY BUD NIPPON

1. Baby Bud Nippon
   incised on doll

BARA
HAND PAINTED
Nippon

2. Bara hand painted Nippon

3. Carpathia M Nippon

4. Cherry blossom hand painted Nippon
   found in blue, green & magenta colors

5. Cherry blossom in a circle
   hand painted Nippon

6. Chikusa hand painted Nippon

7. China E-OH hand painted
   Nippon found in blue & green colors

8. Crown (pointed), hand painted Nippon
   found in green & blue colors

9. Crown Nippon (pointed). Made in Nippon
   found in green and blue colors

10. Crown (square), hand painted Nippon
    found in green and green with red colors

11. Chubby LW & Co. Nippon
found on dolls

15. Double T Diamond in circle Nippon

NIPPON

D

12. D Nippon

16. Dowsie Nippon

13. Dolly sticker found on Nippon's Dolly dolls,
sold by Morimura Bros.

17. EE Nippon

14. Double T Diamond, Nippon

18. Elite B hand painted Nippon

F Y

NIPPON

401

19. FY 401 Nippon
found on dolls

F Y

NIPPON

405

20. FY 405 Nippon
found on dolls

21. G in a circle
hand painted Nippon

Hand painted
GLORIA
L. W. & Co.
NIPPON

22. Gloria L.W. & Co. hand painted
Nippon (Louis Wolf Co., Boston, Mass. & N.Y.C.)

Hand Painted
NIPPON

23. Hand painted Nippon

Hand Painted
Nippon

24. Hand painted Nippon

HAND PAINTED
NIPPON

25. Hand painted Nippon

Hand Painted
NIPPON

26. Hand painted Nippon

Handpainted
NIPPON

27. Hand painted Nippon

28. Hand painted Nippon with symbol

33. Hand painted Nippon with symbol

29. Hand painted Nippon with symbol

30. Hand painted Nippon with symbol

34. Hand painted Nippon with symbol

31. Hand painted Nippon with symbol

35. Hand painted Nippon with symbol

32. Hand painted Nippon with symbol

36. Horsman No. 1 Nippon
    found on dolls

37. IC Nippon

38. Imperial Nippon
found in blue & green

39. JMDS Nippon

40. Jonroth Studio hand painted Nippon

41. Kid Doll M.W. & Co. Nippon

42. Kinjo Nippon

43. Kinjo China hand painted Nippon

44. L & Co. Nippon

45. LFH hand painted Nippon

46. LW & Co. Nippon (Louis Wolf & Co., Boston, Mass & N.Y.C.)

47. M in wreath, hand painted Nippon
(M stands for importer, Morimura Bros.)
found in green, blue, magenta & gold colors

48. M. in wreath hand painted Nippon, D.M. Read Co.
(M stands for importer, Morimura Bros.)

49. M B (Morimura Bros.)
Baby Darling sticker
found on dolls

50. M M hand painted Nippon

MADE IN
NIPPON

51. Made in Nippon

52. Maple leaf Nippon found in green, blue & magenta

53. Morimura Bros.
sticker found on Nippon items

HAND PAINTED

NIPPON

54. Mt. Fujiyama Nippon

NIPPON

55. Nippon
found in blue, gold and also incised into items

NIPPON 84

56. Nippon 84

NIPPON 144

57. Nippon 144

221
NIPPON

58. Nippon 221

59. Nippon with symbol

60. Nippon with symbol

NIPPON

61. Nippon with symbol

NIPPON

62. Nippon with symbol

63. Nippon with symbol

502
NO. 70018

NIPPON

64. Nippon with symbol

NIPPON

M

12

65. Nippon M incised on doll
(note N is written backwards)
#12 denotes size of doll
M = Morimura Bros.

66. Noritake M in wreath Nippon
M = Morimura Bros.
found in green, blue & magenta

67. Noritake Nippon
found in green, blue & magenta colors

68. Noritake Nippon
found in green, blue & magenta colors

69. OAC Hand painted Nippon
(Okura Art China, branch of Noritake Co.)

70. Oriental china Nippon

71. Pagoda hand painted Nippon

PATENT
NO 30441
NIPPON

72. Patent #30441 Nippon

73. Paulownia flowers & leaves
hand painted Nippon (crest used by
Empress of Japan, kiri no mon)
found in a green/red color

74. Paulownia flowers & leaves
hand painted Nippon (crest
used by Empress of Japan, kiri no mon)

75. Pickard etched china, Noritake Nippon
Pickard mark is in black
Noritake/Nippon mark is blue in color

76. Pickard hand painted china Nippon

77. Pickard hand-painted china, Noritake Nippon
Pickard mark printed in black
Noritake Nippon in magenta

78. Queue San Baby Sticker
found on Nippon dolls

79. RC Nippon

80. RC hand painted Nippon
combination of both red & green colors

81. RC Noritake Nippon hand painted
found in green & blue

82. RC Noritake Nippon

Made In Nippon

83. RE Nippon

84. Rising Sun Nippon

ROYAL

NIPPON

85. Royal Dragon Nippon

ROYAL

NIPPON

Studio
Hand Painted

86. Royal Dragon Nippon
Studio hand painted

87. Royal Kaga Nippon

88. Royal Kinran Nippon
found in blue, gold colors

89. Royal Kinran Crown Nippon
found in blue, gold & green colors

90. Royal Moriye Nippon
found in green & blue colors

91. Royal Nishiki Nippon

92. Royal Satsuma Nippon
(cross within a ring, crest of House of Satsuma)

96. S & K hand painted Nippon
found in green, blue & magenta colors

Royal Sometuke
NIPPON

93. Royal Sometuke Nippon

97. S & K hand painted Nippon
found in green, blue & magenta colors

ROYAL SOMETUKE
Nippon
SICILY

94. Royal Sometuke Nippon Sicily

98. Shinzo Nippon

95. R.S. Nippon

99. Shofu Nagoya Nippon

100. SNB Nippon

101. SNB Nagoya Nippon

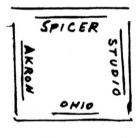

102. Spicer Studio Akron Ohio Nippon
    *(See Page 45)

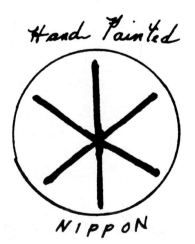

103. Spoke hand painted Nippon

104. Studio hand painted Nippon

105. Superior hand painted Nippon

106. T Nippon
    (2 ho·o birds)

107. T hand painted Nippon

111. TS hand painted Nippon

108. T in wreath hand painted Nippon

112. Teacup Nippon

109. T N hand painted Nippon
mark is red & green

110. TS hand painted Nippon

113. Torii Nippon

114. Tree crest Nippon
(crest of Morimura family)

43

117. Yamato hand painted Nippon

115. Tree Crest & Maple leaf hand painted Nippon

118. Yamato Nippon

116. V Nippon, Scranton, Pa.

119. C.G.N. Hand painted Nippon
found in green

120. F Nippon
03601
600 found incised on dolls

121. F. Nippon
#76012
601 found incised on dolls

F

NO. 76018
NIPPON
30/3

122. F. Nippon
#76018 30/3
found incised on dolls

NO. 76018
NIPPON
403

123. F. Nippon
#76018
403

FY

NIPPON

124. FY Nippon
found incised on dolls

FY

NIPPON
301

125. FY Nippon 301
found incised on dolls

FY

NIPPON
402

126. FY Nippon 402
found incised on dolls.

FY 9

NIPPON
402

127. FY 9 Nippon 402
found incised on dolls

FY

NIPPON
404

128. FY Nippon 404
found incised on dolls

FY

NIPPON
406

129. FY Nippon 406
found incised on dolls

FY

NIPPON
464

130. FY Nippon 464
found incised on dolls

131. FY Nippon
#17604 604
found incised on dolls

132. FY Nippon
#70018 004
found incised on dolls

133. FY Nippon (variation of mark)
#70018 403 found incised on dolls

134. FY Nippon
#70018 406
found incised on dolls

135. FY Nippon (variation of mark)
#70018 406
found incised on dolls

136. FY Nippon
76018
found incised on dolls.

137. Jollikid sticker
(red & white)
found on dolls

138. Ladykin sticker
(red & gold)
found on dolls.

NIPPON

139. Nippon
(notice reversal of first N)
found incised on items

NIPPON
D13495

140. Nippon D13495
found in green

NIPPON
E

141. Nippon E
found incised on dolls

O
NIPPON

142. Nippon O
found incised on dolls

5
NIPPON

143. Nippon 5
found incised on dolls

97
NIPPON

144. Nippon 97
found incised on dolls

98
NIPPON

145. Nippon 98
found incised on dolls

99
NIPPON

146. Nippon 99
found incised on dolls

101
NIPPON

147. Nippon 101
found incised on dolls

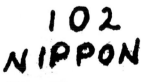
102
NIPPON

148. Nippon 102
found incised on dolls

105 NIPPON

149. Nippon 105
found incised on dolls

123 NIPPON

150. Nippon 123
found incised on dolls

144 NIPPON

151. Nippon 144
with symbol found incised on dolls

152. RE Nippon

153. RE
made in Nippon
found incised on dolls

154. RE Nippon A9
found incised on dolls

155. RE Nippon B8
found incised on dolls

156. RE Nippon
O 2
found incised on dolls

157. Royal Hinode Nippon
found in blue

158. Sonny sticker
(gold, red, white & blue)
found on dolls

159. Maruta Royal Blue Nippon

160. Hand Painted
Coronation Ware
Nippon

BEWARE! The marks shown below are found on reproduction pieces. See section of book dealing with reproduction items.

Numbers found incised on dolls

The majority do not even have numbers, most being just incised with the word NIPPON. In some cases the numbers mean size, height of head, height of doll, circumference of head, etc. 0 is small, 8 is generally of medium size and 18 would be large. Most measurements are in centimeters or millimeters. The largest head would be made from the first model. This new head could be used for a model of the next smaller size, etc. All porcelain shrinks upon drying and firing hence the mold for the head is always larger than the finished product. After size 0 smaller sizes are often denoted by 1/0, 2/0, etc. Numbers found on dolls may also be mold numbers or a code for manufacturers. No hard and fast rule seems to apply.

* According to Jabe Tarter who writes a column on antiques for the Knight-Ridder Newspaper chain, the Spicer Studios were located on Spicer St. in the old Spicer home. The street and village were named for Judge William Spicer and in the years of 1885 to 1915 there were schools of decorating in the area, at the time called Spicer Town. Each class was required to put the name Spicer Studio on their wares but most of the time they were also permitted to place their own name on as the artist as well. The one which was called Spicer rather than Spicer Town as the others were is the best of them all. The paintings on china and porcelain coming from there are avidly sought by collectors of the Akron area. Spicer Town Studios was the owner of the compound. The Spicer Studio was in operation from 1885 to 1910. Mrs. Eva Gifford was the head instructor of the hand painting classes.

Plate 368

Plate 367

Plate 367
    Cobalt scenic vase, 9½″ tall, blue mark #52

Plate 368
    Cobalt scenic vase 9½″ tall, blue mark #52

Plate 369
    Cobalt scenic cracker or cookie jar, 8½″ tall, blue mark #52

Plate 370
    Cobalt scenic vase, 7″ tall, blue mark #52

Plate 371
    Cobalt scenic urn, 17″ tall, blue mark #52

Plate 372
    Cobalt scenic bowls, 7″ diameter, blue mark #52
    Cobalt scenic vase, 10½″ tall, blue mark #52

Plate 369

Plate 370

Plate 371

Plate 372

Plate 373

Plate 373

Cobalt scenic cookie or cracker jar, 8½″ tall, blue mark #52

Plate 374

Cobalt scenic tea set consisting of teapot which is 5½″ tall, creamer, sugar and six cups and saucers, blue mark #52

Plate 375

Cobalt and gold vase, 12½″ tall, blue mark #52

Plate 376

Cobalt scenic cake set, large plate is 10¾″ wide and six small plates are 6¼″ wide, blue mark #52

Plate 377

Cobalt and floral pitcher, 7″ tall, blue mark #52

Plate 378

Cobalt and gold vase, 6½″ tall, blue mark #52
Cobalt scenic vase, 6½″ tall, blue mark #52

Plate 379

Cobalt scenic covered jar, 5″ tall, blue mark #52
Cobalt scenic pitcher, 6¾″ tall, blue mark #52

Plate 374

Plate 375

Plate 376

Plate 377

Plate 378

Plate 379

53

Plate 380

Plate 380
Cobalt scenic plate, 8¾″ wide, blue mark #47
Cobalt scenic plate, 8½″ wide, green mark #47
Plate 381
Cobalt and floral pitcher, 7½″ tall, blue mark #52
Plate 382
Cobalt and floral vase, 14¼″ tall, blue mark #52
Plate 383
Cobalt scenic cake plate, 10¾″ wide, green mark #47
Plate 384
Cobalt scenic vase, 9½″ tall, blue mark #52
Cobalt scenic vase, 9″ tall, blue mark #52
Plate 385
Cobalt and floral plate, 8″ wide, blue mark #52
Plate 386
Cobalt and floral pitcher, 5¾″ tall, green mark #52

Plate 381

Plate 382

Plate 383

Plate 384

Plate 385

Plate 386

Plate 387

Plate 388

Plate 387

   Cobalt and gold plate, 8½″ wide, green mark #47

Plate 388

   Cobalt and floral plates, 7½″ wide, blue mark #52

Plate 389

   Cobalt scenic covered urn, 13¾″ tall, blue mark #114

Plate 390

   Cobalt ewer with heavy gold overlay, 10″ tall, blue mark #52

Plate 391

   Cobalt scenic vase, 13″ tall, green mark #47

Plate 392

   Cobalt and heavy gold overlay humidor, 7½″ tall, blue mark #52

Plate 389

Plate 390

Plate 391

Plate 392

57

Plate 393

Plate 393

Cobalt scenic vase, 13″ tall, blue mark #52

Plate 394

Cobalt and gold chocolate set, pot is 9½″ tall and is marked with the blue mark #52 as well as the four cups and saucers, the matching tray is 12″ in diameter, blue mark #71

Plate 395

Cobalt scenic tankard, 10¼″ tall, blue mark #47

Plate 396

Cobalt scenic vase, 14″ tall, blue mark #52

Plate 397

Cobalt scenic vase, 9″ tall, green mark #47
Cobalt scenic vase, 9½″ tall, green mark #47

Plate 398

Cobalt scenic vase, 12″ tall, green mark #47

Plate 395

Plate 395

Plate 394

Plate 396

Plate 397

Plate 398   59

Plate 399

Plate 399

Cobalt and gold demitasse cups and saucers, each cup is 2″ tall, green mark #47

Plate 400

Cobalt and floral tea set, pot 4½″ tall (see plate #401 for matching cups and saucers), blue mark #52

Plate 401

Cobalt and floral matching cups and saucers to plate #400, blue mark #52

Plate 402

Cobalt and gold tea set, pot is 5½″ tall, set comes with creamer and sugar and eight cups and saucers, blue mark #71

Plate 400

Plate 401

Plate 402

Plate 403

Plate 404

Plate 405

Plate 403

    Tapestry bottle shaped vase, 8½″ tall, blue mark #52

Plate 404

    Tapestry vase, 9½″ tall, blue mark #52

Plate 405

    Tapestry vase, 6″ tall, blue mark #52

Plate 406

    Tapestry vase, 5¼″ tall, blue mark #52

    Tapestry vase, 8″ tall, blue mark #52

    Tapestry vase, 5¼″ tall, blue mark #52

Plate 407

    Tapestry covered urn, 10½″ tall, blue mark #52

Plate 408

    Tapestry vase, 8½″ tall, blue mark #52

Plate 409

    Tapestry ewer, 10¾″ tall, blue mark #52

Plate 406

Plate 407

Plate 408

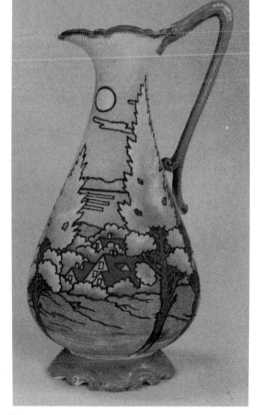

Plate 409

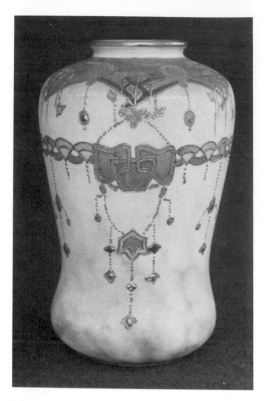

Plate 410

Plate 411

Plate 410
 Tapestry vase, 8″ tall, blue mark #52
Plate 411
 Tapestry vase, 8″ tall, blue mark #52
Plate 412
 Tapestry vase, 9¼″ tall, blue mark #52
 Tapestry basket vase, 8¾″ tall, blue mark #52
Plate 413
 Tapestry vase, 6″ tall, blue mark #52
Plate 414
 Tapestry tankard, 10¾″ tall, blue mark #52
Plate 415
 Tapestry charger, 11¾″ wide, blue mark #52
Plate 416
 Tapestry ewer, 7″ tall, has English hunt scene and Greek key border as design, blue mark #52

Plate 412

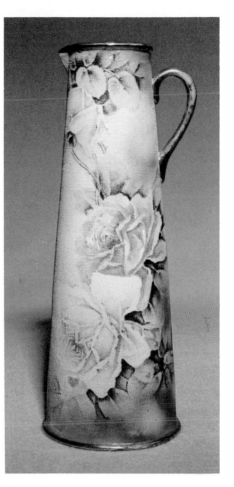

Plate 414

Plate 413

Plate 415

Plate 416

Plate 417

Plate 418

Plate 421

Plate 419

Plate 420

Plate 417

Wedgwood vase, 7½ tall, green mark #47

Plate 418

Wedgwood potpourri jar, 5½" tall, green mark #47

Plate 419

Wedgwood cup and saucer, green mark #47

Plate 420

Wedgwood trimmed creamer and sugar, sugar is 5" tall including the final, green mark #47

Plate 421

Wedgwood ferner having relief molded handles, 8½" wide including handles, green mark #47

Plate 422

Wedgwood vase, 8¾" tall, green mark #47
Wedgwood candlesticks, each 6" tall, green mark #47

Plate 423

Wedgwood trimmed vase, 9" tall, green mark #47

Plate 424

Pair of wedgwood candlesticks, 7½" tall, green mark #47

Plate 425

Wedgwood vase, 8¼" tall, green mark #47

Plate 426

Wedgwood bowl in rare lavender color, 9½" long, green mark #47

Plate 427

Wedgwood slanted cheese dish, 7¾" long, green mark #47

Plate 428

Wedgwood trimmed butter dish (has insert), 6" wide, 3¾" high, green mark #47

Plate 422

Plate 423

Plate 424

Plate 425

Plate 426

Plate 427

Plate 428

67

Plate 429

Plate 430

Plate 431

Plate 432

Plate 433

Plate 429

　　Wedgwood trimmed scenic vase, 11″ tall, green mark #47

Plate 430

　　Wedgwood trimmed floral vase, 8¾″ tall, rare lavender color, green mark #47

Plate 431

　　Wedgwood column ferner, 5″ tall, green mark #47

Plate 432

　　Wedgwood trimmed floral relish dish, 7½″ long, green mark #47

Plate 433

　　Wedgwood ashtray, 3″ tall, green mark #47

Plate 434

　　Wedgwood cup and saucer, blue mark #8

Plate 435

　　Wedgwood trimmed floral vase, 16″ tall, green mark #47

Plate 436

　　Wedgwood ferner, 7″ wide, 3½″ high, green mark #47

Plate 437

　　Wedgwood vase, 9½″ tall, green mark #47

Plate 438

　　Wedgwood trimmed floral bowl, 8¾″ wide including handles, green mark #47
　　Wedgwood trimmed two compartment relish dish, 8½″ wide, green mark #47

Plate 434

Plate 435

Plate 437

Plate 436

Plate 438

Plate 439

Plate 440

Plate 439
Portrait vase, 12″ tall, blue mark #52
Plate 440
Portrait vase, 7″ tall, blue mark #52
Plate 441
Portrait urn, 12″ tall, blue mark #52
Plate 442
Pair of portrait vases, 10″ tall, blue mark #52
Plate 443
Portrait vase, 12″ tall, blue mark #52
Plate 444
Portrait humidor, 7¾″ tall, blue mark #52
Plate 445
Portrait dresser tray, 12″ long, blue mark #52

Plate 441

Plate 442

Plate 443

Plate 444

71

Plate 445

Plate 448

Plate 446   Plate 447

Plate 446
  Portrait vase, 9½″ tall, blue mark #52
Plate 447
  Portrait covered urn, 9½″ tall, blue mark #52
Plate 448
  Portrait mug, 5½″ tall, green mark #47
Plate 449
  Portrait plaque, 10″ diameter, green mark #42
Plate 450
  Portrait plaque, 10″ diameter, green mark #52
Plate 451
  Portrait vase, 9½″ tall, blue mark #52
Plate 452
  Portrait vase, 9″ tall, has some moriage trim, blue mark #52
Plate 453
  Portrait stein, 7″ tall, green mark #47
Plate 454
  Portrait vase, 12″ tall, blue mark #52
Plate 455
  Portrait plaque, 9½″ tall, green mark #47
Plate 456
  Portrait wine jugs, each 9½″ tall, blue mark #52

Plate 449

Plate 450

Plate 451

Plate 452

Plate 453

late 454

Plate 455

Plate 456

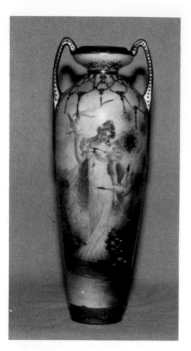

Plate 458

Plate 457

Plate 457

Portrait vase, 12½" tall, blue mark #52

Plate 458

Portrait candlestick, 9" tall, blue mark #52

Plate 459

Portrait vase 12" tall, blue mark #52

Plate 460

Portrait covered urn, 10½" tall, blue mark #52

Plate 461

Portrait vase, 18¼" tall, blue mark #52

Plate 462

Portrait creamer and sugar, sugar is 3½" tall including finial, green mark #52

Plate 463

Portrait vase, 7" tall, blue mark #52

Plate 464

Portrait ewer, 6½" tall, green mark #52

Plate 465

Portrait vase, 9" tall, blue mark #52
Portrait vase, 8¾" tall, blue mark #52

Plate 459

Plate 460

Plate 461

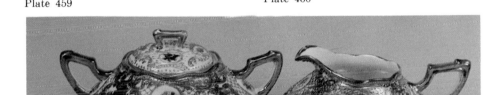

Plate 462

Plate 463

Plate 464

Plate 465

Plate 466

Plate 467

Plate 468

Plate 469

Plate 466

Moriage vase, 9¼″ tall, mark #70

Plate 467

Moriage vase, 7½″ tall, blue mark #47

Plate 468

Moriage tankard, 12″ tall, blue mark #52

Plate 469

Moriage vase, 5″ wide, 2″ tall, blue mark #52

Plate 470

Moriage vase, 7″ tall, green mark #52
Moriage vase, 9½″ tall, blue mark #52

Plate 471

Moriage vase, 9″ tall, 9″ wide, blue mark #52

Plate 472

Moriage creamer and sugar, sugar is 4¼″ tall including finial, green mark #90
Moriage vase, 7″ tall, green mark #90

Plate 473

Moriage vase, 8½″ wide, 3″ high, blue mark #52

Plate 474

Moriage vase, 7″ tall, blue mark #52

Plate 475

Moriage vase, 8½″ tall, green mark #52

Plate 470

Plate 471

Plate 472

Plate 473

Plate 474

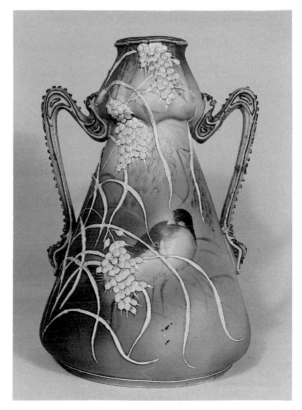

Plate 475

77

Plate 477

Plate 476

Plate 476

    Moriage vase, 9¼" tall, blue mark #52

Plate 477

    Moriage vase, 7" tall, green mark #52

Plate 478

    Moriage two piece urn, 11" tall, blue mark #90

    Moriage tankard, 10" tall, blue mark #52

Plate 479

    Moriage vase, also molded in relief, 6" tall, green mark #47

Plate 480

    Moriage ferner, also molded in relief, 6" wide, green mark #47

Plate 481

    Moriage tankard, 14¼" tall, blue mark #52

Plate 482

    Moriage covered urn, 11" tall, green mark #52

Plate 483

    Moriage vase, 8½" tall, green mark #52

Plate 484

    Moriage vase, also molded in relief, 9½" tall, green mark #47

Plate 478

Plate 481

Plate 479

Plate 480

Plate 482

Plate 483

Plate 484

Plate 486

Plate 485

Plate 487

Plate 488

Plate 485

Moriage vase, 5¼″ tall, blue mark #70

Plate 486

Moriage vase, 6½″ tall, blue mark #52

Plate 487

Moriage teapot, 6½″ tall, green mark #71

Plate 488

Moriage creamer, 5″ tall, blue mark #52

Plate 489

Moriage vase, 10½″ tall, blue mark #52

Plate 490

Moriage vase, 13½″ tall, blue mark #52

Plate 491

Moriage vase, 10″ tall, green mark #52

Plate 492

Moriage vase, note jeweling on butterfly's wings, 9″ tall, blue mark #52

Plate 493

Moriage vase, 9″ tall, blue mark #90

Plate 494

Moriage vase, 12½″ tall, blue mark #52

Plate 495

Moriage vase, 6″ tall, blue mark #52
Moriage vase, 7″ tall, green mark #52

Plate 496

Moriage ewer, 7½″ tall, blue mark #47
Moriage hanging plaque, 7¾″ diameter, blue mark #47

Plate 489

Plate 490

Plate 491

Plate 492

Plate 493

Plate 494

Plate 495

Plate 496

81

Plate 497

Plate 498

Plate 497
  Moriage chocolate set, pot is 9″ tall, set comes with five cups and saucers, green mark #47
Plate 498
  Moriage pitcher, 6″ tall, blue mark #52
Plate 499
  Moriage tankard, 15¾″ tall, mark #70
Plate 500
  Moriage ewer, 9″ tall, mark #24
Plate 501
  Moriage pitcher, 7″ tall, blue mark #52
Plate 502
  Moriage mug, 5½″ tall, blue mark #52
Plate 503
  Moriage ewer, 7½″ tall, blue mark #90
Plate 504
  Moriage vase, 8¼″ tall, blue mark #52
Plate 505
  Moriage humidor, 8″ tall, blue mark #52
  Moriage wine jug, 8″ tall, blue mark #52

Plate 499

Plate 500

Plate 501

Plate 503

Plate 502

Plate 504

Plate 505

83

Plate 506

Plate 508

Plate 507

Plate 506

Moriage vase, 8½″ tall, blue mark #52

Plate 507

Moriage sugar and creamer, sugar bowl is 4½″ tall including finial, mark #16

Plate 508

Moriage hanging plaque, 9½″, green mark #52

Plate 509

Moriage lemonade set consisting of pitcher which is 6½″ tall and five cups which are 3¾″ tall, green mark #101

Plate 510

Moriage vase, 5½″ tall, green mark #52

Plate 511

Moriage cracker or cookie jar, 8″ tall, blue mark #52

Plate 512

Moriage tea set, pot is 5½″ tall including finial, set includes creamer, sugar and six cups and saucers, green mark #47

Plate 513

Moriage covered urn, 14½″ tall, blue mark #52

Plate 514

Moriage tea set, pot is 6¾″ tall with finial, set consists of teapot, sugar, creamer and six cups and saucers, mark #73

Plate 509

Plate 510

Plate 511

Plate 512

Plate 513

Plate 514

85

Plate 515

Plate 516

Plate 518

Plate 517

Plate 519

Plate 520

Plate 521

Plate 515
   Moriage vase, 9″ tall, blue mark #90
Plate 516
   Moriage vase, 8¾″ tall, blue mark #90
Plate 517
   Moriage vase, 3½″ tall, 5½″ in diameter, blue mark #90
Plate 518
   Moriage compote, 5″ wide including handles, blue mark #90
   Moriage vase, 4¾″ tall, blue mark #90
Plate 519
   Moriage vases, 6″ tall, green mark #47
Plate 520
   Moriage creamer and sugar, sugar bowl is
   3½″ tall with finial, green mark #47

Plate 521
   Moriage vase, 6″ tall, green mark #52
Plate 522
   Moriage vase, 7″ tall, green mark #90
   Moriage humidor, 6½″ tall, blue mark #90
Plate 523
   Moriage humidor, also molded in relief, 6½″ tall, green mark #47
Plate 524
   Moriage ashtray, 5½″ wide, green mark #47
   Moriage mug, 5½″ tall, green mark #47
Plate 525
   Moriage ashtray, 5¼″ wide, green mark #47
Plate 526
   Moriage vase, 12½″ tall, green mark #47
   Moriage vase, 8½″ tall, blue mark #52
Plate 527
   Moriage tea set, pot is 6¾″ tall, creamer is 3¾″ tall and sugar is 5″ tall including finial, green mark #71

Plate 522

Plate 523

Plate 524

Plate 525

Plate 526

Plate 527

Plate 528

Plate 529

Plate 530

Plate 531

Plate 528
    Molded in relief hanging plaque, 12″ wide, green mark #47
Plate 529
    Molded in relief humidor, 6½″ tall, green mark #47
Plate 530
    Molded in relief sugar and creamer set, sugar bowl is 4½″ tall including finial, green mark #47
Plate 531
    Molded in relief humidor, 7½″ tall, mark #47
Plate 532
    Molded in relief humidor, 7″ tall, green mark # 47
Plate 533
    Molded in relief humidor, 6¾″ tall, green mark #47
Plate 534
    Molded in relief humidor, 7¼″ tall, green mark #47
Plate 535
    Molded in relief humidor, 7¼″ tall, green mark #47

Plate 532

Plate 533

Plate 534

Plate 535

Plate 537

Plate 536

Plate 538

Plate 536

    Top row, nut bowl molded in relief, 7¾″ wide, green mark #47

    Bottom row, nut bowl molded in relief, 8¾″ wide, green mark #47

Plate 539

Plate 537

    Molded in relief humidor, 6¼″ tall, (see plate #'s 539 & 545 for different decoration of same mold) green mark #47

Plate 538

    Molded in relief nut bowl, 8½″ wide, green mark #47

    Molded in relief nut bowl, 8½″ wide, green mark #47

Plate 539

    Molded in relief humidor, 6¼″ tall, (see plate #'s 537 & 545 for different decoration of same mold), green mark #47

Plate 540

    Molded in relief humidor, 6¼″ tall, blue mark #110

Plate 541

    Molded in relief humidor, 7¼″ tall, green mark #47

Plate 542

    Molded in relief humidor, 7¼″ tall, green mark #47

Plate 543

    Molded in relief humidor, 6½″ tall, green mark #47

Plate 544

    Molded in relief humidor, 6½″ tall, green mark #47

Plate 545

    Molded in relief humidor, 6¼″ tall, (see plate #'s 537 & 539 for different decoration of same mold,) green mark #47

Plate 540

Plate 541

Plate 542

Plate 543

Plate 544

Plate 545

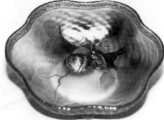

Plate 546
Plate 547
Plate 549

Plate 548
Plate 551
Plate 550

Plate 546

    Top row, molded in relief nut bowl, 4½″ wide, green mark #47

    Bottom row, molded in relief nut bowl, 7½″ wide, green mark #47

Plate 547

    Top row, molded in relief nut bowl, 7½″ wide, green mark #47

    Bottom row, molded in relief nut bowl, 7½″ wide, green mark #47

Plate 548

    Molded in relief humidor, 7½″ tall, green mark #47

Plate 549

    Molded in relief vase, 8″ tall, (see front view in plate #553), green mark #47

Plate 550

    Molded in relief humidor, 7½″ tall, blue mark #52

Plate 551

    Molded in relief ashtray, 5¼″ wide, (see plate #555 for different decoration of same mold), green mark #47

Plate 552

    Molded in relief humidor, 7½″ tall, green mark #47

Plate 553

    Molded in relief vase, 8″ tall, (see rear view in plate #549), green mark #47

Plate 554

    Molded in relief hanging plaque, 10″ in diameter, green mark #47

Plate 555

    Molded in relief ashtrays, 5¼″ wide, (see plate #551 for different decoration of same mold), green mark #47

Plate 556

    Molded in relief hanging plaque, 10″ in diameter, green mark #47

Plate 557

    Molded in relief hanging plaque, 10½″ in diameter, green mark #47

Plate 552

Plate 553

Plate 554

Plate 555

Plate 556

Plate 557

93

Plate 558

Plate 559

Plate 560

Plate 561

Plate 562

Plate 563

Plate 558

    Molded in relief rose bowl, 3½″ high, green mark #47

Plate 559

    Molded in relief vase, 9¾″ tall, green mark #47

Plate 560

    Molded in relief vase, 12½″ tall, blue mark #52

Plate 561

    Molded in relief nut bowl, 5¾″ wide, green mark #47

Plate 562

    Molded in relief nut bowl, 7″ wide, green mark #47

Plate 563

    Molded in relief nut bowl, 7½″ wide including handles, green mark #47

Plate 564

    Molded in relief vase, 8½″ vase, blue mark #52

Plate 565

    Molded in relief vase, 10½″ tall, green mark #47

Plate 566

    Molded in relief wine jug, 11″ tall, green mark #47

Plate 567

    Molded in relief vase, 7″ tall, blue mark #52

Plate 568

    Molded in relief charger, 13½″ wide, green mark #47

Plate 569

    Molded in relief basket, 7½″ wide, green mark #47
    Molded in relief vase, 7½″ tall, green mark #47

Plate 570

    Molded in relief combination ashtray and matchbox holder, 5¼″ long and 4½″ tall, green mark #47

Plate 564

Plate 565

Plate 566

Plate 567

Plate 568

Plate 569

Plate 570

Plate 571   Plate 572

Plate 571
    Heavily beaded decanter, 7″ tall, mark #10
Plate 572
    Heavily beaded cookie or cracker jar, 7″ tall, 8″ wide, blue mark #52
Plate 573
    Heavily beaded vase, 7½″ tall, green mark #52
Plate 574
    "Sponge" tapestry vase, 8¼″ tall, blue mark #52
Plate 575
    "Sponge" tapestry vase, 8½″ tall, blue mark #52
Plate 576
    Heavily beaded vase, 7¼″ tall, unmarked
Plate 577
    Heavily beaded vase, 6″ tall, blue mark #52
Plate 578
    Heavily beaded berry set, large bowl is 10½″ in diameter, small bowls are 5″ in diameter, blue mark #52
Plate 579
    Heavily beaded candlestick, 10¾″ tall, blue mark #52

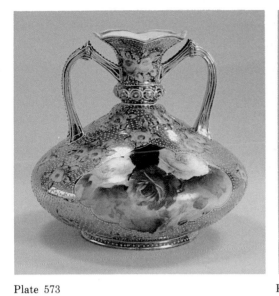

Plate 573

Plate 574

Plate 575

Plate 576

Plate 577

Plate 578

Plate 579

97

Plate 580

Plate 581

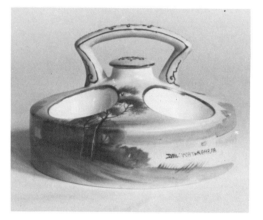

Plate 582

Plate 583

Plate 584

Plate 580

Imitation Gouda style bowl, 8″ wide, green mark #47

Plate 581

Compote supported by three griffins, base is triangular in shape, 8″ wide, 5″ tall, green mark #47

Plate 582

Souvenir egg warmer, says Watergap, Pa. on it, 5½″ wide, green mark #47

Plate 583

Three piece sardine set with figural sardine sprigged on top, 6¼″ long, green mark #47

Plate 584

Figural bird, 4¼″ tall, green mark #47

Plate 585

Coralene vase, 9½″ tall, mark #95

Plate 586

Souvenir "Nipper" figural, says "Souvenir of Colorado Springs, Colo.", 4½″ long, green mark #26

Plate 587

Four piece bridge ashtray set, each approximately 4″ wide, blue mark #84

Plate 588

Figural bunny light, 6¼″ tall, green mark #47
Figural owl light, 6¼″ tall, green mark #47

Plate 589

Figural matchbox holder, 3″ tall, incised with mark #55

Plate 590

Figural tea set consisting of pot which is 4″ tall including finial, creamer, sugar and six cups and saucers, green mark #47

Plate 585

Plate 586

Plate 587

Plate 588

Plate 589

Plate 590

Plate 591

Plate 592

Plate 593

Plate 594

Plate 591

      Top row, figural monkey, 4½″ tall, mark #55

      Bottom row, figural bird, 5″ long, green mark #47

              figural bird toothpick holder, 3″ tall, green mark #47

              figural bird, 4½″ long, green mark #47

Plate 592

      Figural of three monkeys, "see no evil, hear no evil, speak no evil," 4″ wide, 2½″ high, incised with mark #55

Plate 593

      Figural owl and tree bookend, one of a pair, 9″ tall, green mark #47

Plate 594

      Figural seal ashtray, tray is 7″ long, seal is 3½″ tall, green mark #47

Plate 595

      Figural ashtray, 6″ wide, green mark #47

Plate 596

      Figural penguin ashtray, 6″ across, 5″ tall, green mark #47

Plate 597

      Figural fox ashtray, 6½″ long, green mark #47

Plate 598

      Figural dog ashtray and combination matchbox holder, 5″ wide, 4″ deep, green mark #47

Plate 599

      Figural pipe ashtray, 4½″ wide, green mark #47

Plate 600

      Figural kingfisher ashtray, 6½″ wide, green mark #47

Plate 595

Plate 596

Plate 597

Plate 598

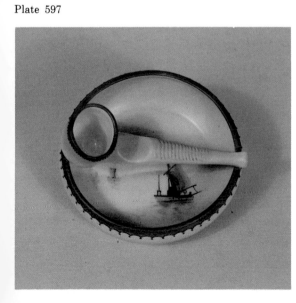

Plate 599

Plate 600

101

Plate 601

Plate 602

Plate 603

Plate 604

Plate 601

    Figural bird on small dish, 6″ wide, blue mark #84

    Figural egg trinket box with heavy moriage trim, 6″ long, green mark #47

    Figural lion on side of ashtray, 4½″ wide, green mark #47

Plate 602

    Figural boy ashtray, 3½″ wide, 2½″ tall, blue mark #84

Plate 603

    Figural incense burner, 6″ tall, mark #55

    Figural incense burner, 8″ tall, mark #55

    Figural incense burner, 5″ tall, mark #55

Plate 604

    Figural bird on relish dish, 7¾″ wide, green mark #47

Plate 605

    Doll, 24″ tall, mark #133

Plate 606

    Doll, 20″ tall, mark #123

Plate 607

    Doll, 15″ tall, mark #121

Plate 608

    Doll, 24″ tall, mark #128

Plate 609

    Doll, 15½″ tall, mark #133

Plate 605

Plate 606

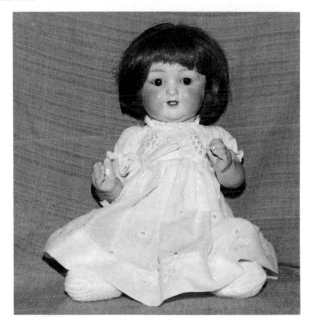

Plate 607

Plate 608

Plate 609

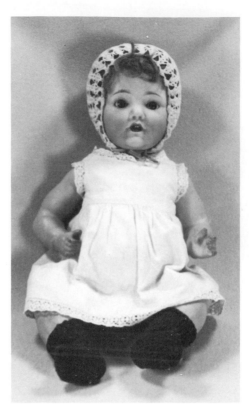

Plate 611

Plate 612

Plate 610

Plate 610
    Doll, 24″ tall, mark #153
Plate 611
    Doll, 13″ tall, mark #155
Plate 612
    Doll, 12″ tall, mark #121
Plate 613
    Doll, 12″ tall, mark #122
Plate 614
    Doll, 9″ tall, mark #55
Plate 615
    Doll, 4½″ tall, mark #55
Plate 616
    Twin dolls, 3½″ tall, mark #55
Plate 617
    Doll, 5″ tall, mark #144
    Doll, 5¼″ tall, mark #147
Plate 618
    Doll, 9″ tall, mark #55

Plate 613

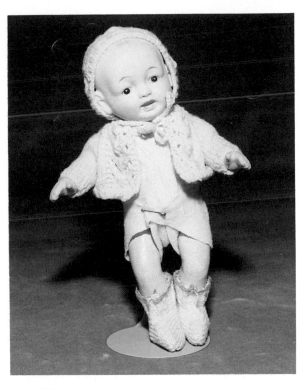

Plate 614

Plate 615

Plate 616

Plate 617

Plate 618

105

Plate 619

Plate 620

Plate 621

Plate 622

Plate 619

    Doll, 4¾″ tall, mark #55
    Doll, 4¾″ tall, mark #55

Plate 620

    Doll, 6″ tall, mark #55

Plate 621

    Doll, 5″ tall, mark #55

Plate 622

    Doll, 4¼″ tall, mark #55
    Doll, 3¾″ tall, mark #55

Plate 623

    Doll, 5½″ tall, mark #55
    Doll, 4″ tall, mark #55

Plate 624

    Doll, 4″ tall, mark #55

Plate 625

    Doll, 6″ tall, mark #55
    Doll, 6½″ tall, mark #55

Plate 626

    Doll, 5″ tall, mark #55
    Doll, 5¼″ tall, mark #55

Plate 627

    Doll, 5¼″ tall, mark #55
    Doll, 4¼″ tall, mark #55

Plate 628

    Doll, 5″ tall, mark #55

Plate 623

Plate 624

Plate 625

Plate 626

Plate 627

Plate 628

Plate 629

Plate 630

Plate 631

Plate 632

Plate 629
    Doll, 4½″ tall, mark #55
Plate 630
    Doll, 4¾″ tall, mark #55
    Doll, 4¾″ tall, mark #55
Plate 631
    Dolly doll with original sticker (#13), 3½″ tall, mark #55
    Doll, 3¼″ tall, mark #55
Plate 632
    Doll, 3¾″ tall, mark #55
Plate 633
    Doll, 6¾″ tall, mark #55
    Doll, 7″ tall, mark #55
Plate 634
    Doll, 6¼″ tall, mark #55
    Doll, 5¾″ tall, mark #55
Plate 635
    Doll, 4¼″ tall, mark #55
    Doll, 7″ tall, cloth body, mark #55
Plate 636
    Doll, 6½″ tall, mark #55
    Doll, 6½″ tall, mark #55
Plate 637
    Doll, 5¼″ tall, mark #55
Plate 638
    Doll, 5″ tall, mark #55
    Doll, 4″ tall, mark #55

Plate 633

Plate 634

Plate 635

Plate 636

Plate 637

Plate 638

109

Plate 639

Plate 640

Plate 639
    Doll, 4¼″ tall, mark #55
    Doll, 3¼″ tall, mark #55
Plate 640
    Doll, 4¼″ tall, mark #55
    Doll, 5¼″ tall, mark #55
Plate 641
    Doll, 4½″ tall, mark #55
    Doll, 4½″ tall, mark #55
Plate 642
    Doll, 5″ tall, mark #55
    Doll, 7¼″ tall, mark #55
Plate 643
    Doll, 5½″ tall, mark #55
Plate 644
    Doll, 4½″ tall, mark #55
Plate 645
    Doll, 4½″ tall, mark #55
    Doll, 4½″ tall, mark #55
Plate 646
    Doll, 4½″ tall, mark #55

Plate 641

Plate 642

Plate 643

Plate 644

Plate 645

Plate 646

111

Plate 647

Plate 648

Plate 649

Plate 647
   Doll, 4″ tall, mark #55
Plate 648
   Dolls, smaller ones are 3¾″ tall, larger is 5¾″ tall, mark #55
Plate 649
   Doll, 6″ tall, mark #55
Plate 650
   Doll, 3½″ tall, mark #55
Plate 651
   Doll, 5½″ tall, mark #55
   Doll, 6½″ tall, mark #55
Plate 652
   Doll, 4½″ tall, mark #55
   Doll, 4¾″ tall, mark #55
Plate 653
   Doll, 3½″ tall, mark #55
Plate 654
   Doll, 4¼″ tall, mark #55
   Doll, 4½″ tall, mark #55
Plate 655
   Twin dolls, 4½″ tall, mark #55
Plate 656
   Large Baby Bud doll, 7″ tall, mark #55
Plate 657
   Doll, 4½″ tall, mark #55

Plate 650

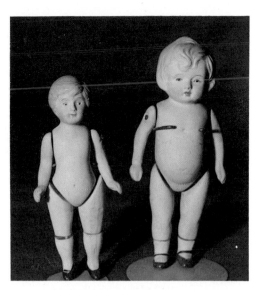

Plate 651

Plate 652

Plate 653

Plate 654

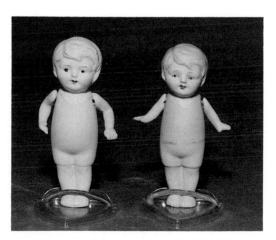

Plate 655

Plate 656

Plate 657

113

Plate 658

Plate 659

Plate 658
   Baby doll with bottle, jointed arm allows bottle to go in mouth, 3½″ tall, mark #55
Plate 659
   Doll 5″ tall, mark #55
   Doll, 4½″ mark #55
Plate 660
   Doll, 4¾″ tall, mark #55
Plate 661
   Doll, 5¼″ tall, mark #55
Plate 662
   Doll, 3¾″ tall, mark #55
   Doll, 3¾″ tall, mark #55
Plate 663
   Doll, 5″ tall, mark #55
   Kewpie doll, 5″ tall, mark #55
Plate 664
   Doll, 4¾″ tall, mark #55
   Doll, 5″ tall, mark #55
Plate 665
   Ballerina doll, 3¼″ tall, mark #55
Plate 666
   Twin dolls, 4¼″ tall, mark #55
Plate 667
   Twin dolls, one dressed, one undressed, 5″ tall, mark #144
Plate 668
   Baby doll with bottle, jointed arm allows bottle to go in mouth, 5½″ tall, mark #55

Plate 660

Plate 661

Plate 662

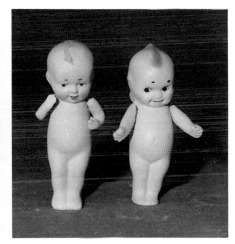

Plate 663

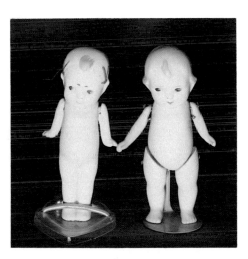

Plate 664

Plate 665

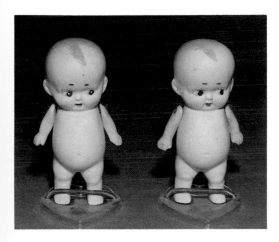

Plate 666

Plate 667

Plate 668

115

Plate 670

Plate 671

Plate 669

Plate 669

    Kewpie doll 5¾″ tall, mark #55

Plate 670

    Doll, 4¾″ tall, mark #55
    Doll, 5″ tall, mark #145

Plate 671

    Doll, 4¾″ tall, mark #55
    Doll, 4½″ tall, mark #55

Plate 672

    Doll, 5¼″ tall, mark #146
    Doll, 5½″ tall, mark #55

Plate 673

    Queue San Baby, 5″ tall, has sticker #78 on front, mark #55
    Sonny doll, has sticker #158 on front, mark #55

Plate 674

    Doll, 4″ tall, mark #55
    Doll, 4¼″ tall, mark #55

Plate 675

    Doll, 4½″ tall, mark #55
    Doll, 5″ tall, mark #55

Plate 676

    Doll in bathtub, doll is 1¾″ long, 2½″ tall, tub is 3″ long, 1½″ tall, both are incised with mark #55

Plate 677

    Kewpie doll, 4¼″ tall, has red and gold sticker saying "Kewpie, Reg. U.S. Off.," mark #55
    Kewpie doll, 5¼″ tall, had red and gold sticker saying "Kewpie, Reg. U.S. Off.," mark #55

Plate 678

    Doll in bathtub, doll is 1½″ tall, tub is 2½″ long, tub is incised with mark #55

Plate 679

    Same as #678

Plate 672

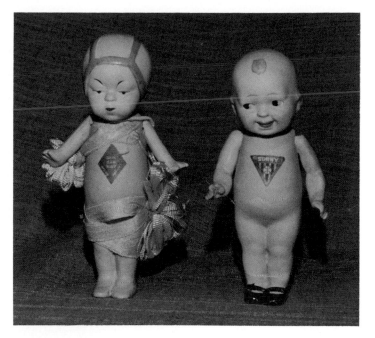

Plate 673

Plate 674

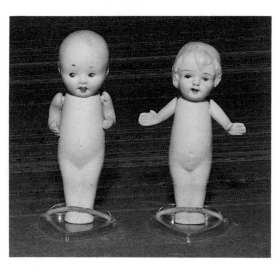

Plate 675

Plate 676

Plate 677

Plate 678

Plate 679

117

Plate 680

Plate 681

Plate 682

Plate 683

Plate 680

    Doll, 6″ tall, mark #55

    Doll, 5¾″ tall, mark #55

Plate 681

    Doll, 6″ tall, mark #58

    Doll, 5½″ tall, mark #141

Plate 682

    Half doll with sew holes, 2½″ tall, mark #55

    Half doll with sew holes, 2½″ tall, mark #55

Plate 683

    Child's dresser set, hatpin holder is 2″ tall, blue mark #84

Plate 684

    Ladykin doll, 3½″ tall, has sticker #138, mark #55

Plate 685

    Rear view of plate #684 showing sticker

Plate 686

    Rear view of Jollikid doll, 3¾″ tall, has sticker #137, mark #55

Plate 687

    Doll head, 1¾″ tall, mark #55

Plate 688

    Doll head, 1¾″ tall, mark #55

Plate 689

    Front view of Jollikid doll, plate #686

Plate 690

    Child's play tea set, consists of teapot, creamer, sugar, four cups and saucers and plates, pot is 4″ tall, blue mark #84

Plate 684

Plate 685

Plate 686

Plate 687

Plate 688

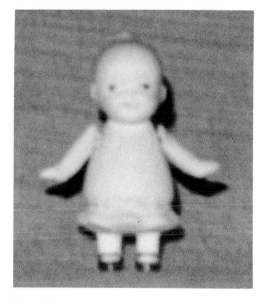

Plate 689

Plate 690

119

Plate 691

Plate 692

Plate 693

Plate 694

Plate 691

Child's feeding dish, 7″ wide, blue mark #84

Plate 692

Child's play tea set, consists of teapot, creamer, sugar, four cups and saucers, pot is 3½″ tall, blue mark #84

Plate 693

Child's play tea set, consists of teapot, creamer, sugar, six cups and saucers and plates, pot is 3¼″ tall, cups are 1½″ tall, blue mark #84

Plate 694

Child's feeding dishes consisting of a plate, 6½″ wide, cup which is 2½″ tall and a creamer which is 3¼″ tall, all have blue mark #84

Plate 695

Child's play tea set depicting Sunbonnet Babies, consists of teapot, creamer, sugar, six cups and saucers and plates, blue mark #66

Plate 696

Child's egg cup, 2½″ tall, blue mark #84

Plate 697

Child's play tea set, consists of teapot, creamer, sugar, four cups and saucers and plates, blue mark #84

Plate 698

Child's dresser set, each item 2¾″ wide, green mark #47

Plate 699

Child's play tea set consisting of teapot, creamer, sugar, six cups, saucers and plates, blue mark #84

Plate 700

Child's play tea set consisting of teapot, creamer, sugar, four cups, saucers and plates, blue mark #84

Plate 701

Child's candlestick, 5½″ tall, green mark #47

Plate 695

Plate 696

Plate 697

Plate 698

Plate 699

Plate 701

Plate 700

121

Plate 702

Plate 703

Plate 704

Plate 705

Plate 702

Child's feeding dish, 7″ wide, green mark #8

Plate 703

Child's feeding set consisting of feeding dish which is 6¾″ wide, plate which is 6½″ wide, bowl which is 4¾″ wide and creamer which is 3″ tall, blue mark #84

Plate 704

Child's play creamer and sugar set, sugar bowl is 2½″ tall including finial, blue mark #84

Plate 705

Child's play creamer and sugar set, sugar bowl is 3″ tall including finial, mark #10

Plate 706

Child's chamberstick, 1½″ tall, green mark #47

Plate 707

Child's play tea set consisting of teapot, creamer, sugar and four cups, saucers and plates, teapot is 4″ tall, blue mark #84

Plate 708

Child's play tea set consisting of teapot which is 3½″ tall, creamer, sugar and four cups, saucers and plates, blue mark #84

Plate 709

Child's dresser set, tray is 6″ long and 4″ wide, hatpin holder is 1¾″ tall and hair receiver is 2½″ wide, mark #113

Plate 710

Child's play tea set consisting of teapot which is 3½″ tall, creamer, sugar and six cups, saucers and plates, blue mark #84

Plate 711

Child's feeding dish, 8″ wide, blue mark #84

Plate 706

Plate 707

Plate 708

Plate 709

Plate 710

Plate 711

123

Plate 712

Plate 713

Plate 714

Plate 712

Small dish from tea set, 4¾″ wide, green mark #8

Plate 713

Child's mug, 2½″ tall, blue mark #84

Plate 714

Doll face patterned items, on left is tiny tea set, cups are 1″ in diameter by 1″ tall, saucers are 1⅝″ wide, the creamer is 1¼″ tall, the sugar is 1⅝″ tall and the teapot is 2⅞″ tall, blue mark #55 is incised on bottom

On right side is bigger tea set, the cups are 1¼″ tall and 1¼″ in diameter, the saucers are 2½″ in diameter, the covered sugar is 2½″ tall and the teapot is 3¼″ tall, blue mark #55 is incised on bottom of pieces

Plate 715

Doll face patterened items, child's breakfast set, fruit bowl is 5¼″ wide, the egg cup is 3½″ tall, the cereal bowl is 5¾″ wide, mug is 2¾″ tall, plate is 5¾″ wide and the creamer is 3″ tall, all marked with blue mark #84

Plate 716

Doll face patterned items, on left is powder box which is 4″ across and 3″ tall, on right is heart shaped dish which is 5¼″ wide, both have blue mark #84

Plate 717

Doll face patterned hanging plaque, 6⅛″ wide, blue mark #84

Plate 718

Doll face patterned mugs, largest is 3″ in diameter, medium one is 2¾″ wide and the smallest is 2½″ wide, all have blue mark #84

Plate 719

Doll face patterned cup and saucer, cup is 2⅛″ tall and saucer is 5″ wide, blue mark #84

Plate 715

Plate 716

Plate 717

Plate 718

Plate 719

Plate 720

Plate 721

Plate 722

Plate 723

Plate 720

    American Indian decorated ashtray, 5¼″ diameter, green mark #47
    American Indian decorated humidor, 4″ tall, green mark #47
    American Indian decorated nappy, 5½″ in diameter, green mark #47

Plate 721

    American Indian decorated creamer, 2½″ tall, green mark #47
    American Indian decorated ashtray, 4¾″ wide, green mark #47

Plate 722

    American Indian decorated vase, 14″ tall, green mark #47

Plate 723

    American Indian decorated hanging plaque, 10½″ wide, blue mark #52

Plate 724

    American Indian decorated molded in relief humidor, 6½″ tall, green mark #47

Plate 725

    American Indian decorated humidor, 5½″ tall, green mark #47

Plate 726

    American Indian decorated molded in relief ashtray, 6½″ long, green mark #47

Plate 727

    American Indian decorated ashtray, 5½″ wide, green mark #47

Plate 728

    American Indian decorated molded in relief ferner, 6¾″ tall, 6″ wide, green mark #47

Plate 729

    American Indian decorated molded in relief humidor, 7¾″ tall, green mark #47

Plate 724

Plate 725

Plate 726

Plate 727

Plate 728

Plate 729

127

Plate 730

Plate 731

Plate 732

Plate 733

Plate 734

Plate 730

    Wine jug, Indian in canoe, 8¾" tall, green mark #47

Plate 731

    Cracker jar, Indian in canoe, 8½" diameter, green mark #47

Plate 732

    Vase, Indian in canoe, 7" tall, green mark #47

Plate 733

    Tea set consisting of teapot, creamer, sugar, and six cups and saucers, Indian in canoe pattern, pot is 4½" tall, green mark #109

Plate 734

    Nut dish, Indian in canoe, 5½" wide, green mark #47

Plate 735

    Hanging plaque, 11" wide, green mark #47

Plate 736

    Humidor, 6" tall, green mark #47

Plate 737

    Vase, Indian in canoe, 12½" tall, blue mark #52

Plate 738

    Ferner, Indian in canoe, 8" long, green mark #47

Plate 739

    Celery dish, Indian in canoe, 12" long, green mark #47

Plate 740

    Hanging plaque, 10" wide, green mark #47

Plate 735

Plate 736

Plate 737

Plate 738

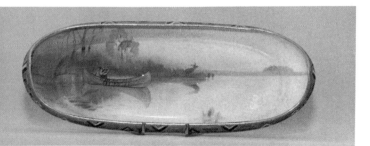

Plate 739

Plate 740

Plate 741

Plate 742

Plate 743

Plate 744

Plate 741

Two tier serving dish, 8½″ wide, Indian in canoe, mark #17

Plate 742

Bowl, Indian in canoe, 7½″ wide, green mark #47

Plate 743

Hanging plaque, man on camel scene, 10″ wide, green mark #47

Plate 744

Three piece inkwell set, has insert, man on camel scene, 2¾″ wide, green mark #47

Plate 745

Stein, man on camel scene, 7″ tall, green mark #47

Plate 746

Vase, man on camel scene, 9″ tall, green mark #47
Vase, man on camel scene, 7″ tall, green mark #47

Plate 747

Pair of vases, man on camel scene, 6″ tall, green mark #47

Plate 748

Vase, man on camel scene, 18″ tall, green mark #47

Plate 749

Hanging plaque, man on camel scene, 10″ wide, green mark #47
Hanging plaque, man on camel scene, 10″ wide, green mark #47

Plate 750

Mug, man on camel scene, some moriage trim, 4¾″ tall, green mark #47

Plate 745

Plate 746

Plate 747

Plate 748

Plate 749

Plate 750

131

Plate 752

Plate 751

Plate 751

Vase, man on camel scene, 18″ tall, green mark #47

Plate 752

Cigarette box, man on camel scene, 4½″ long, green mark #47

Plate 753

Vase, man on camel scene, some moriage trim, 12½″ tall, green mark #47

Plate 754

Chocolate set, man on camel scene, consists of chocolate pot which is 9½″ tall and four cups and saucers, green mark #47

Plate 755

Fruit bowl, man on camel scene, 12″ wide, green mark #47

Plate 756

Vase, man on camel scene, 8″ tall, blue mark #52

Plate 757

Cookie or cracker jar, man on camel scene, 8½″ tall, green mark #47

Plate 758

Vase, man on camel scene, 9″ tall, green mark #47

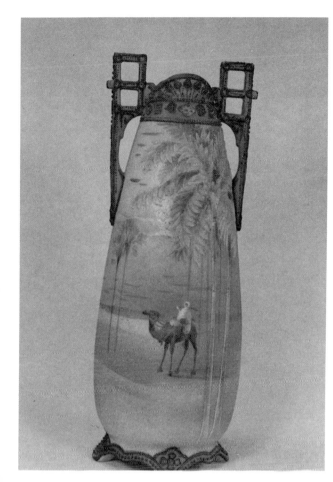

Plate 753

Plate 754

Plate 755

Plate 756

Plate 757

Plate 758

Plate 759   Plate 760

Plate 761

Plate 759
    Candy dish, hunt scene, 12″ long, blue mark #52
Plate 760
    Mug, hunt scene, 4¾″ tall, green mark #47
Plate 761
    Bon bon dish, hunt scene, 5½″ wide, green mark #47
Plate 762
    Humidor, hunt scene, 7¼″ tall, blue mark #47
Plate 763
    Wine jug, hunt scene, 9½″ tall, blue mark #52
Plate 764
    Vase, hunt scene, 9¼″ tall, green mark #47
Plate 765
    Cracker jar, hunt scene, 9½″ wide, 5″ tall, blue mark #52
Plate 766
    Hanging plaque, hunt scene, 9½″ wide, green mark #47
Plate 767
    Hanging plaque, hunt scene, 10″ wide, green mark #47

Plate 762

Plate 763

Plate 764

Plate 765

Plate 766

Plate 767

135

Plate 768

Plate 769

Plate 770   Plate 771   Plate 772   Plate 773

Plate 768

Woodland scene chocolate set consisting of pot which is 10¼″ tall and four cups and saucers, green mark #47

Plate 769

Woodland scene compote, 6½″ wide, 3½″ high, green mark #47

Plate 770

Woodland scene after-dinner coffee set consisting of a tray which is 12″ in diameter, pot is 6½″ tall, creamer is 3″ tall and sugar bowl is 3½″ tall including finial, green mark #47

Plate 771

Woodland scene wine jug, 9½″ tall, blue mark #52

Plate 772

Woodland scene ewer, 6½″ tall, blue mark #52

Plate 773

Woodland scene vase, 6¼″ tall, blue mark #52

Plate 774

Woodland scene tea set consisting of tray which is 12″ in diameter, teapot which is 6″ tall, creamer, sugar and six cups and saucers, mark #119

Plate 775

Woodland scene hanging plaque, 10″ wide, green mark #52

Plate 776

Woodland scene hanging plaque, 10″ wide, green mark #47

Plate 777

Woodland scene small compote, 5″ wide including handles, green mark #47

Plate 778

Woodland scene salt and pepper shaker set, each piece is 2½″ tall, green mark #47
Matching mustard pot, 2¾″ tall, green mark #47

Plate 774

Plate 775

Plate 776

Plate 777

Plate 779

Plate 780

Plate 781

Plate 779

Humidor, 5″ tall, decorated with mythological griffins which are animals with the body and hind legs of a lion and the head and wings of an eagle, blue mark #47

Plate 780

Humidor, 6″ tall, green mark #47
Humidor, 6¾″ tall, green mark #47
Humidor, 6″ tall, green mark #47

Plate 781

Humidor, 6½″ tall, green mark #47

Plate 782

Humidor, 5½″ tall, green mark #47

Plate 783

Humidor, has some moriage trim, 6″ tall, green mark #47

Plate 784

Humidor, 5½″ tall, green mark #47
Humidor, 6″ tall, green mark #47

Plate 785

Humidor, 6″ tall, green mark #47

Plate 786

Humidor, 5½″ tall, green mark #52
Humidor, 6¾″ tall, blue mark #52
Humidor, has verison of hunt scene as decor, 6″ tall, blue mark #52

Plate 787

Humidor, 6½″ tall, green mark #47

Plate 782

Plate 783

Plate 784

Plate 785

Plate 786

Plate 787

Plate 788

Plate 789

Plate 790   Plate 791

Plate 788
    Humidor, 5¾″ tall, green mark #47
    Ashtray, 3¼″ diameter, green mark #47
Plate 789
    Humidor, 6″ tall, blue mark #47
Plate 790
    Humidor, 6½″ tall, green mark #47
Plate 791
    Humidor, 5″ tall, green mark #47
Plate 792
    Humidor, 7″ tall, green mark #47
Plate 793
    Humidor, 5½″ tall, green mark #47
Plate 794
    Humidor, 4″ tall, green mark #47
Plate 795
    Humidor, 7″ tall, green mark #47
Plate 796
    Humidor, 7″ tall, blue mark #52
Plate 797
    Humidor, 6¾″ tall, green mark #47
Plate 798
    Humidor, 7¼″ tall, green mark #47

Plate 792

Plate 793

Plate 794

Plate 795

Plate 796

Plate 797

Plate 798

141

Plate 799

Plate 800

Plate 801

Plate 802

Plate 799

  Humidor, 5″ tall, some moriage trim, green mark #47

Plate 800

  Humidor, 7½″ tall, green mark #47

Plate 801

  Ashtray, 5″ wide, green mark #47

Plate 802

  Ashtray, 4¼″ wide, blue mark #84

Plate 803

  Humidor, 6½″ tall, green mark #47

Plate 804

  Ashtray, 4¾″ long, green mark #47

Plate 805

  Humidor, 6″ tall, green mark #47

Plate 806

  Ashtray, 4½″ wide, green mark #47
  Ashtray, 5½″ wide, green mark #47
  Ashtray, 4½″ wide, green mark #47

Plate 807

  Humidor, figural of squirrel is finial, 8″ tall, blue mark #52

Plate 808

  Ashtray, 5½″ wide, green mark #47
  Ashtray, 6″ wide, green mark #47
  Ashtray, 5½″ wide, green mark #47

Plate 809

  Ashtray, 4¾″ wide, green mark #47
  Ashtray, 4¾″ wide, green mark #47
  Ashtray, 4¾″ wide, green mark #47

Plate 803

Plate 804

Plate 805

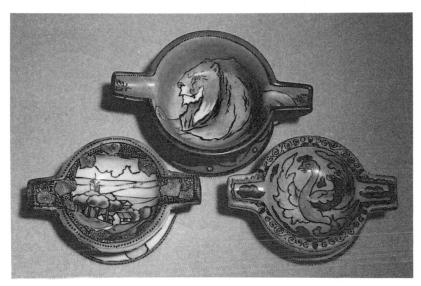

Plate 806

Plate 807

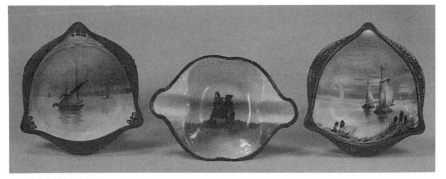

Plate 808

Plate 809

143

Plate 810

Plate 811

Plate 812

Plate 813

Plate 814

Plate 810

    Combination matchbox holder and ashtray, 3½″ tall, blue mark #47

Plate 811

    Ashtray, 6¼″ wide, green mark #47

Plate 812

    Combination matchbox holder and ashtray, 3½″ tall, blue mark #47

Plate 813

    Ashtray, 5″ wide, green mark #47

Plate 814

    Cigarette box, 4½″ long, green mark #47

Plate 815

    Ashtray, 5¼″ wide, green mark #47

    Ashtray, 5¼″ wide, green mark #47

Plate 816

    Ashtray, 5½″ wide, green mark #47

Plate 817

    Combination matchbox holder and ashtray, 3″ tall, green mark #47

    Combination matchbox holder and ashtray, 3½″ tall, green mark #47

Plate 818

    Combination matchbox holder and ashtray, 4¾″ tall, green mark #47

Plate 819

    Hanging double matchbox holder, 6″ long, green mark #47

    Hanging single matchbox holder, 4½″ long, green mark #47

Plate 820

    Combination matchbox holder and ashtray, 4½″ tall, green mark #47

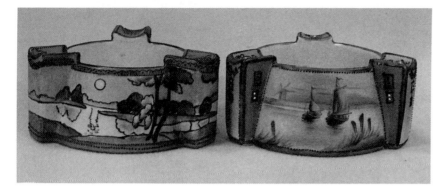

Plate 815

Plate 816

ate 817

Plate 818

Plate 819

Plate 820

145

Plate 821

Plate 822

Plate 823

Plate 821
    Four piece smoke set, tray is 7¾″ wide, green mark #47
Plate 822
    Four piece smoke set, tray is 7½″ wide, green mark #47
Plate 823
    Four piece smoke set, tray is 6¾″ wide, green mark #47
Plate 824
    Ashtray, 4″ wide, green mark #47
Plate 825
    Six piece smoke set, tray is 11½″ long, blue mark #3
Plate 826
    Cigar box, 5½″ long, green mark #47
Plate 827
    Three piece smoke set, tray is 7″ wide, green mark #47
Plate 828
    Cigarette box, 4½″ long, green mark #47
    Cigarette box, 4½″ long, green mark #47
Plate 829
    Four piece smoke set, tray is 7″ in diameter, green mark #47

Plate 824

Plate 825

Plate 827

Plate 829

Plate 831

Plate 830

Plate 832

Plate 833

Plate 830

Ladies' desk set, tray is 8½″ long, and 5¼″ wide, green mark #47

Plate 831

Inkwell with pen rest, 3½″ tall, green mark #47

Plate 832

Stein, 7″ tall, green mark #47

Plate 833

Stein, 7″ tall, green mark #47

Plate 834

Inkwell with tray, also has pen rest, tray is 5½″ long, green mark #47

Plate 835

Desk set, blotter corner is 4″ long, ink blotter is 4½″ long, envelope holder is 3″ high, inkwell is 4″ wide and the tray is 8½″ long, green mark #47

Plate 836

Inkwell with tray which has pen rest, tray is 5½″ long, green mark #47

Blotter is 4½″ long, green mark #47

Plate 837

Inkwell, 3″ wide, green mark #47

Plate 838

Stamp box portraying hoo bird, 2¾″ long, green mark #47

Plate 839

Ladies' desk set, stamp box is 3″ long, inkwell is 3½″ tall, envelope holder is 4″ tall and the blotter is 4½″ long, green mark #47

Plate 834

Plate 835

Plate 836

Plate 837

Plate 838

Plate 839

Plate 840

Plate 841

Plate 842

Plate 843

Plate 840
     Mug, 5½" tall, green mark #47
Plate 841
     Mug, 5½" tall, green mark #47
Plate 842
     Mug, 4½" tall, green mark #47
Plate 843
     Mug, 5½" tall, green mark #47
Plate 844
     Mug, 5½" tall, green mark #47
     Mug, 5½" tall, green mark #47
Plate 845
     Mug, 5" tall, green mark #47
Plate 846
     Mug, 5" tall, gold mark #47
Plate 847
     Mug, 5" tall, green mark #47
     Mug, 5½" tall, green mark #47
Plate 848
     Tankard set, tankard is 11" tall, comes with six mugs which are 4¾" tall, has some moriage trim, green mark #47
Plate 849
     Stein, 7" tall, green mark #47

Plate 844

Plate 845

Plate 846

Plate 847

Plate 848

Plate 849

151

Plate 851

Plate 850

Plate 852

Plate 850

    Tankard, 14¾″ tall, green mark #26

Plate 851

    Mug, 5¾″ tall, green mark #47

Plate 852

    Tankard, 14½″ tall, green mark #52

Plate 853

    Tankard, 14″ tall, blue mark #52

Plate 854

    Tankard set, tankard is 11″ tall, five mugs are 4¾″ tall, green mark #47

Plate 855

    Tankard set, tankard is 11″ tall, four mugs are 4¾″ tall, green mark #47

Plate 853

Plate 851

Plate 855

153

Plate 858

Plate 857

Plate 856

Plate 856
    Wine jug, 9½″ tall, green mark #47
Plate 857
    Wine jug, 8¼″ tall, green mark #47
Plate 858
    Whiskey jug, 8″ tall, blue mark #52
Plate 859
    Wine jug, 11″ tall, has some moriage trim, blue mark #47
Plate 860
    Whiskey jug, 7½″ tall, green mark #47
    Whiskey jug, 7½″ tall, blue mark #52
Plate 861
    Whiskey jug, 7½″ tall, blue mark #52
    Whiskey jug, 7″ tall, green mark #52
Plate 862
    Whiskey jug, 6½″ tall, green mark #47
Plate 863
    Whiskey jug, 7½″ tall, green mark #47
    Whiskey jug, 7½″ tall, green mark #47
Plate 864
    Wine jug, 7¾″ tall, green mark #47

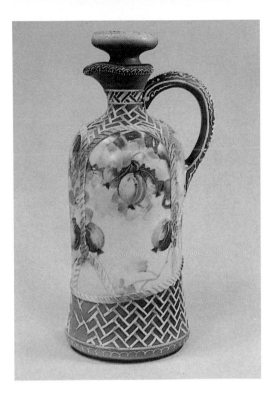

Plate 859

Plate 860

Plate 861

Plate 862

Plate 863

Plate 864

155

Plate 865

Plate 866

Plate 867

Plate 865
Hanging plaque, 12″ wide, green mark #47
Plate 866
Hanging plaque, 10″ wide, green mark #47
Plate 867
Hanging plaque, 10″ wide, green mark #47
Plate 868
Hanging plaque, 10¼″ wide, green mark #47
Plate 869
Hanging plaque, 10¼″ wide, green mark #47
Plate 870
Hanging plaque, 12″ wide, artist signed, green mark #47
Plate 871
Hanging plaque, 11″ wide, green mark #47
Plate 872
Hanging plaque, 10″ wide, green mark #47
Plate 873
Hanging plaque, 12″ wide, green mark #47

Plate 868

Plate 869

Plate 870

Plate 871

Plate 872

Plate 873

Plate 874

Plate 875

Plate 876

Plate 877

Plate 874
   Hanging plaque, 9″ wide, green mark #47
Plate 875
   Hanging plaque, 9″ wide, green mark #47
Plate 876
   Hanging plaque, 10″ wide, blue mark #52
Plate 877
   Hanging plaque, 10″ wide, blue mark #52
Plate 878
   Hanging plaque, 11″ wide, green mark #47
Plate 879
   Hanging plaque, 7¾″ wide, blue mark #52

Plate 880
   Hanging plaque, 8½″ wide, blue mark #52
Plate 881
   Hanging plaque, 10″ wide, blue mark #52
Plate 882
   Hanging plaque, 11″ wide, green mark #47
Plate 883
   Hanging plaque, 10″ wide, green mark #47
Plate 884
   Hanging plaque, 11″ wide, blue mark #52
   Hanging plaque, 10″ wide, green mark #47

Plate 878

Plate 879

Plate 880

Plate 881

Plate 882

Plate 883

Plate 884

Plate 885

Plate 886

Plate 887

Plate 888

Plate 885

    Hanging plaque, 10″ wide, green mark #47

Plate 886

    Hanging plaque, 10″ wide, green mark #47

Plate 887

    Hanging plaque, 10″ wide, green mark #47

Plate 888

    Hanging plaque, 7½″ wide, some moriage trim, green mark #47

Plate 889

    Hanging plaque, 11″ wide, green mark #47

Plate 890

    Hanging plaque, 8¾″ wide, green mark #47

Plate 891

    Hanging plaque, 10″ wide, green mark #47
    Hanging plaque, 10″ wide, green mark #47

Plate 892

    Hanging plaque, 9″ wide, green mark #47

Plate 893

    Hanging plague, 10″ wide, green mark #47
    Hanging plaque, 10″ wide, green mark #47

Plate 894

    Hanging plaque, 10″ wide, blue mark #52

Plate 889

Plate 890

Plate 891

Plate 892

Plate 893

Plate 894

Plate 895

Plate 896

Plate 897

Plate 898

Plate 895
> Hanging plaque, 10″ wide, green mark #47

Plate 896
> Hanging plaque, 10″ wide, green mark #47

Plate 897
> Hanging plaque, 10″ wide, green mark #47

Plate 898
> Hanging plaque, 10″ wide, green mark #47

Plate 899
> Hanging plaque, 7¾″ wide, green mark #47

Plate 900
> Hanging plaque, 7½″ wide, green mark #47

Plate 901
> Hanging plaque, 7¾″ wide, green mark #47

Plate 902
> Hanging plaque, 10″ wide, green mark #47

Plate 903
> Hanging plaque, 7½″ wide, blue mark #47
> Hanging plaque, 7½″ wide, green mark #47

Plate 904
> Hanging plaque, 9½″ wide, green mark #47

Plate 899

Plate 900

Plate 901

Plate 902

Plate 903

Plate 904

163

Plate 905

Plate 906

Plate 907

Plate 908

Plate 905

    Hanging plaque, 10″ wide, green mark #47

Plate 906

    Hanging plaque, 10″ wide, green mark #47

Plate 907

    Hanging plaque, 10″ wide, green mark #47

Plate 908

    Hanging plaque, 10″ wide, green mark #47

Plate 909

    Hanging plaque, 10″ wide, green mark #47

Plate 910

    Hanging plaque, 10″ wide, green mark #47

Plate 911

    Hanging plaque, 7¾″ wide, blue mark #52

Plate 912

    Hanging plaque, 10″ wide, green mark #47

Plate 913

    Hanging plaque, 10″ wide, green mark #47

Plate 914

    Hanging plaque, 10″ wide, green mark #47

Plate 909

Plate 910

Plate 911

Plate 912

Plate 913

Plate 914

165

Plate 915

Plate 916

Plate 917

Plate 915
>   Hanging plaque, 11″ wide, some moriage trim, green mark #47

Plate 916
>   Hanging plaque, 10″ wide, green mark #47

Plate 917
>   Hanging plaque, 10″ wide, green mark #47

Plate 918
>   Hanging plaque, 11″ wide, green mark #47
>   Hanging plaque, 10″ wide, green mark #47

Plate 919
>   Hanging plaque, 10″ wide, green mark #47

Plate 920
>   Hanging plaque, 9″ wide, green mark #47

Plate 921
>   Hanging plaque, 10½″ wide, green mark #47

Plate 922
>   Hanging plaque, 10″ wide, green mark #47
>   Hanging plaque, 11″ wide, green mark #47

Plate 923
>   Hanging plaque, 10″ wide, green mark #47

Plate 918

Plate 919

Plate 920

Plate 921

Plate 922

Plate 923

Plate 924

Plate 925

Plate 926

Plate 927

Plate 928

Plate 924

Hanging plaque, 9″ wide, green mark #47

Plate 925

Hanging plaque, 10″ wide, green mark #47

Plate 926

Hanging plaque, 10″ wide, green mark #47

Plate 927

Hanging plaque, 10″ wide, green mark #47

Plate 928

Hanging plaque, 10″ wide, green mark #47

Plate 929

Hanging plaque, 6″ wide, green mark #47

Plate 930

Hanging plaque, 11″ wide, green mark #47

Plate 931

Hanging plaque, 9¼″ wide, blue mark #52

Plate 932

Hanging plaque, 11″ wide, blue mark #47

Plate 933

Hanging plaque, 10″ wide, green mark #47

Plate 934

Hanging plaque, 9″ wide, green mark #47

Plate 929

Plate 930

Plate 931

Plate 932

Plate 933

Plate 934

Plate 935

Plate 936

Plate 937

Plate 935
   Vase, 10″ tall, blue mark #52
Plate 936
   Vase, 12″ tall, blue mark #52
Plate 937
   Vase, 9″ tall, green mark #47
Plate 938
   Vase, 9½″ tall, green mark #47
Plate 939
   Vase, 10½″ tall, green mark #47
Plate 940
   Vase, 12¾″ tall, blue mark #52
Plate 941
   Vase, 13″ tall, blue mark #52
Plate 942
   Vase, 8½″ tall, blue mark #47
Plate 943
   Vase, 9½″ tall, green mark #47
Plate 944
   Vase, 10½″ tall, blue mark #52

Plate 938

Plate 939

Plate 940

Plate 941

Plate 942

Plate 943

Plate 944

171

Plate 945

Plate 946

Plate 945

    Vase, 8½″ tall, green mark #52

    Vase, 6¼″ tall, green mark #47

Plate 946

    Vase, 10½″ tall, blue mark #52

Plate 947

    Vase, 16½″ tall, blue mark #52

Plate 948

    Vase, 6¼″ tall, man on camel scene, green mark #47

    Vase, 8″ tall, green mark #47

Plate 949

    Vase, 15″ tall, green mark #52

Plate 950

    Vase, 8½″ tall, green mark #47

    Vase, 8½″ tall, green mark #47

Plate 951

    Pair of vases, 10¾″ tall, blue mark #52

Plate 952

    Vase, 13½″ tall, green mark #47

    Vase, 13½″ tall, same mold as first, different decoration, green mark #47

Plate 953

    Vase, 10½″ tall, green mark #52

Plate 954

    Vase, 13″ tall, blue mark #47

Plate 947

Plate 948

Plate 949

Plate 950

Plate 951

Plate 952

Plate 953

Plate 954

173

Plate 955

Plate 956

Plate 957

Plate 958

Plate 955
    Vase, 7½″ tall, green mark #47
    Vase, 7¼″ tall, green mark #47

Plate 956
    Pair of vases, 7¾″ tall, green mark #47

Plate 957
    Vase, 8″ tall, green mark #47

Plate 958
    Pair of vases, some moriage trim, each 9″ tall, blue mark #52

Plate 959
    Vase, 8″ tall, some moriage trim, blue mark #52

Plate 960
    Basket vase, 6″ high, 7¼″ wide, green mark #47

Plate 961
    Vase, 7½″ tall, blue mark #52

Plate 962
    Ewer, 6¾″ tall, blue mark #52

Plate 963
    Ewer, 12½″ tall, blue mark #52

Plate 964
    Vase, 10¾″ tall, green mark #52

Plate 965
    Vase, 13″ tall, blue mark #47

Plate 966
    Vase, 8″ tall, blue mark #52

Plate 959

Plate 960

Plate 961

Plate 962

Plate 963

Plate 964

Plate 965

Plate 966

175

Plate 967

Plate 968

Plate 969

Plate 967
  Vase, 10½″ tall, green mark #47
Plate 968
  Vase, 6½″ tall, green mark #47
  Vase, 6½″ tall, green mark #47
Plate 969
  Pair of vases, 9″ tall, green mark 47
Plate 970
  Vase, 9″ tall, blue mark #52
Plate 971
  Vase, 9½″ tall, green mark #47
  Vase, 8″ tall, green mark #47
Plate 972
  Vase, 10″ tall, green mark #52
  Tankard, 10¼″ tall, blue mark #52
Plate 973
  Vase, 8″ tall, blue mark #52
Plate 974
  Ewer, 13″ tall, blue mark #52
Plate 975
  Vase, 11¼″ tall, green mark #52

Plate 970

Plate 971

Plate 972

Plate 973

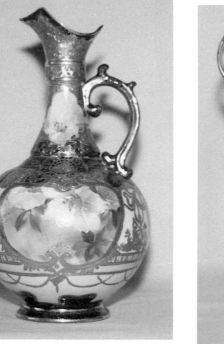

Plate 974

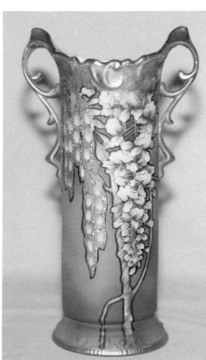

Plate 975

177

Plate 976

Plate 977

Plate 978

Plate 976
    Vase, 13″ tall, green mark #47

Plate 977
    Vase, 8¾″ tall, green mark #47

Plate 978
    Vase, 11½″ tall, green mark #47

Plate 979
    Vase, 13½″ tall, green mark #47
    Vase, 13¾″ tall, green mark #47

Plate 980
    Pair of vases, 14″ tall, green mark #47

Plate 981
    Vase, 13¾″ tall, green mark #47
    Vase, 13″ tall, green mark #47

Plate 982
    Vase, 7″ tall, green mark #47
    Vase, 8″ tall, gold overlay, man on camel scene, green mark #47

Plate 983
    Vase, 8½″ tall, green mark #47
    Vase, 8¼″ tall, green mark #47

Plate 984
    Vase, 10½″ tall, green mark #47
    Vase, 10½″ tall, green mark #47

Plate 979

Plate 980

Plate 981

Plate 982

Plate 983

Plate 984

179

Plate 985

Plate 986

Plate 987

Plate 988

Plate 989

Plate 985
    Vase, 11″ tall, green mark #47
Plate 986
    Vase, 9½″ tall, green mark #47
Plate 987
    Vase, 8½″ tall, green mark #47
Plate 988
    Pair of urns (two pieces bolted together), 8¼″ tall, green mark #47
Plate 989
    Vase, 6″ tall, blue mark #38
    Bon bon dish, 5″ wide, blue mark #38
    Vase, 7″ tall, blue mark #38
Plate 990
    Vase, 13″ tall, green mark #47

Plate 991
    Vase, 13″ tall, unmarked
Plate 992
    Vase, 7″ tall, green mark #47
Plate 993
    Vase, 10″ tall, blue mark #47
    Vase, 9½″ tall, green mark #47
Plate 994
    Vase, 15″ tall, green mark #47
Plate 995
    Vase, 6¾″ tall, blue mark #38
    Vase, 6¾″ tall, pattern stamped, green mark #47

Plate 990

Plate 991

Plate 992

Plate 993

Plate 994

Plate 995

181

Plate 996

Plate 997

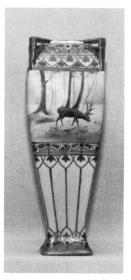

Plate 998

Plate 999

Plate 996
Vase, 9½″ tall, (reverse side of plate #1002), mark #91

Plate 997
Pair of vases, 10¼″ tall, unmarked

Plate 998
Vase, 12″ tall, green mark #47

Plate 999
Vase, 12½″ tall, green mark #47

Plate 1000
Vase, 8″ tall, blue mark #52

Plate 1001
Vase, 8½″ tall, blue mark #47

Plate 1002
Vase, 9½″ tall, mark #91 (see reverse side in plate #996)

Plate 1003
Vase, 8″ tall, blue mark #52

Plate 1004
Vase, 14″ tall, green mark #47

Plate 1005
Ewer, 12¼″ tall, blue mark #52

Plate 1000

Plate 1001

Plate 1003

Plate 1002

Plate 1004

Plate 1005

183

Plate 1007

Plate 1008

Plate 1006

Plate 1009

Plate 1006
> Vase, 6½″ tall, green mark #47

Plate 1007
> Vase, 10″ tall, blue mark #17

Plate 1008
> Vase, 13″ tall, green mark #47

Plate 1009
> Vase, 3″ tall, green mark #47
> Vase, 4½″ tall, green mark #47
> Vase, 2½″ tall, green mark #47
> Vase, 2½″ tall, green mark #47

Plate 1010
> Vase, 12″ tall, blue mark #52
> Vase, 10″ tall, blue mark #52

Plate 1011
> Vase, 7½″ tall, has heavy gold trim, green mark #47

Plate 1012
> Vase, 10″ tall, blue mark #47
> Vase, 11″ tall, green mark #47

Plate 1013
> Vase, 13″ tall, green mark #47

Plate 1014
> Vase, 10¼″ tall, blue mark #47

Plate 1015
> Vase, 12″ tall, blue mark #52

Plate 1016
> Vase, 9¾″ tall, green mark #47
> Vase, 8¾″ tall, green mark #47

Plate 1017
> Vase, 7½″ tall, blue mark #47
> Vase, 8½″ tall, blue mark #47

Plate 1010

Plate 1011

Plate 1012

Plate 1013

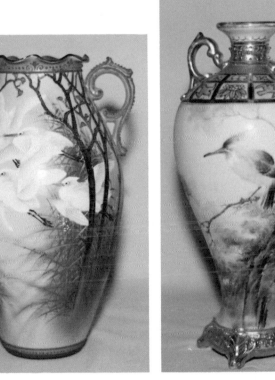

Plate 1014

Plate 1015

Plate 1016

Plate 1017

185

Plate 1018

Plate 1019

Plate 1020

Plate 1021

Plate 1018
   Vase, 8″ tall, green mark #47
Plate 1019
   Vase, 9½″ tall, blue mark #52
Plate 1020
   Vase, 9¼″ tall, green mark #47
Plate 1021
   Vase, 6″ tall, blue mark #52
   Vase, 6″ tall, blue mark #47
Plate 1022
   Vase, 14″ tall, green mark #47
Plate 1023
   Vase, 12″ tall, green mark #47
Plate 1024
   Vase, 14″ tall, green mark #47
Plate 1025
   Vase, 13″ tall, green mark #47
Plate 1026
   Pair of vases, each 13″ tall, green mark #47

Plate 1022

Plate 1023

Plate 1024

Plate 1025

Plate 1026

Plate 1027

Plate 1028

Plate 1029

Plate 1027
    Vase, 9¾″ tall, green mark #47
Plate 1028
    Pair of vases, 7¼″ tall, mark #55
Plate 1029
    Vase, 10″ tall, blue mark #52
Plate 1030
    Vase, 10″ tall, green mark #52
Plate 1031
    Covered urn, 13″ tall, green mark #52
Plate 1032
    Vase, 11″ tall, blue mark #47
Plate 1033
    Vase, 5¾″ tall, green mark #47
Plate 1034
    Vase, 7¼″ tall, green mark #47
Plate 1035
    Vase, 6½″ tall, green mark #47

Plate 1032

Plate 1030

Plate 1031

Plate 1033

Plate 1034

Plate 1035

189

Plate 1037

Plate 1036

Plate 1036
    Covered urn, 9″ tall, blue mark #52
Plate 1037
    Covered urn, 11″ tall, mark #89
Plate 1038
    Large urn, 24½″ tall, blue mark #52
Plate 1039
    Large urn, 20¾″ tall, blue mark #52
Plate 1040
    Covered urn, 14″ tall, blue mark #52
Plate 1041
    Urn, 12″ tall, green mark #47
Plate 1042
    Urn, 15″ tall, blue mark #47
Plate 1043
    Covered urn, 14¼″ tall, green mark #47

Plate 1038

Plate 1039

Plate 1040

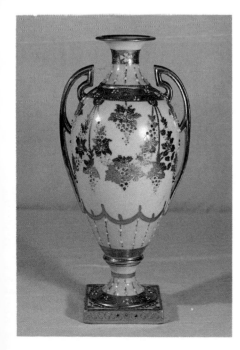

Plate 1041

Plate 1042

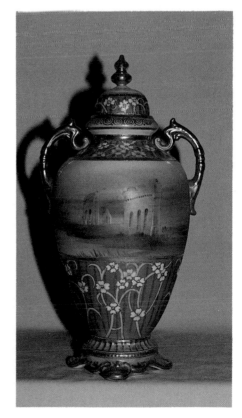

Plate 1043

Plate 1044

Plate 1045

Plate 1046

Plate 1044

Column ferner, 5″ tall, green mark #47

Plate 1045

Ferner, 8½″ wide with relief molded handles, 3¾″ high, green mark #47

Plate 1046

Ferner, 6¾″ wide, green mark #47

Plate 1047

Hanging pot, 5″ tall, 4″ wide, blue mark #47

Plate 1048

Hanging pot, 5″ tall, 4″ wide, green mark #47

Plate 1049

Ferner, 9½″ long, green mark #47
Ferner, 7½″ long, green mark #47

Plate 1050

Ferner, 8″ long, green mark #47
Ferner, 6¾″ long, green mark #47

Plate 1051

Hanging pot, 5″ tall, green mark #47

Plate 1052

Hanging pot, 5″ tall, green mark #47
Hanging pot, 5″ tall, green mark #47

Plate 1053

Hanging pot, 5″ tall, green mark #47

Plate 1047

Plate 1048

Plate 1049

Plate 1050

Plate 1051

Plate 1052

Plate 1053

Plate 1054

Plate 1055

Plate 1054
    Cookie or cracker jar, 7″ high, green mark #47
Plate 1055
    Cookie or cracker jar, 8¼″ tall, green mark #52
Plate 1056
    Ferner, 8½″ wide including relief molded handles, green mark #47
Plate 1057
    Ferner, 6″ wide, 3¼″ tall, green mark #47
Plate 1058
    Ferner, 8½″ wide including relief molded handles, green mark #47
Plate 1059
    Cookie or cracker jar, 8½″ tall, green mark #47
Plate 1060
    Cracker jar, 8″ wide, 6″ high, green mark #47
Plate 1061
    Cookie or cracker jar, 7½″ tall, green mark #52
Plate 1062
    Cookie or cracker jar, 8½″ tall, green mark #47
Plate 1063
    Cookie or cracker jar, 7″ tall, green mark #47

Plate 1056

Plate 1057

Plate 1058

Plate 1059

Plate 1060

Plate 1061

Plate 1062

Plate 1063

195

Plate 1064

Plate 1065

Plate 1064

Cracker jar, 7″ wide, mark #80

Cracker jar, 7″ wide, blue mark #52

Plate 1065

Cracker or cookie jar, 7″ tall, blue mark #52

Plate 1066

Punch set, punch bowl is 16″ wide including handles, cups are 4″ tall, green mark #47

Plate 1067

Punch set, punch bowl is 9½″ wide, cups are 3¾″ high, green mark #47

Plate 1066

Plate 1067

Plate 1068

Plate 1069

Plate 1068

Game platter and sauce dish (see plate #'s 1069, 1072 & 1073 for rest of set), platter is 17″ long, green mark #47

 Sauce dish, is 6½″ long, green mark #47

Plate 1069

Two game plates, matching #1068, each 8½″ wide, green mark #47

Plate 1070

Game set consists of 16½″ platter and six plates, green mark #47

Plate 1071

Fish set consists of 17½″ platter and five plates 9″ long, green mark #24

Plate 1070

Plate 1071

Plate 1072

Plate 1073

Plate 1072

Game plates, match platter in plate #1068, each is 8½″ wide, green mark #47

Plate 1073

Game plates, match platter in plate #1068, each is 8½″ wide, green mark #47

Plate 1074

Game platter, 17″ long, green mark #47

Plate 1075

After dinner coffee set consisting of pot and four cups and saucers, pot is 9″ tall, blue mark #52

Plate 1076

Chocolate set consisting of 8¾″ pot, four cups and saucers, mark #80

Plate 1077

Chocolate set consisting of pot 11″ tall and four cups and saucers, cups are 3″ tall, blue mark #52

Plate 1078

Chocolate pot, 10¼″ tall, blue mark #52

Plate 1074

Plate 1075

Plate 1076

Plate 1077

Plate 1078

Plate 1079

Plate 1080

Plate 1081

Plate 1082

Plate 1079

Chocolate set consisting of chocolate pot, 9″ tall, and six cups and saucers, green mark #47

Plate 1080

Chocolate set consists of chocolate pot which is 10¾″ tall and four cups and saucers, mark #80

Plate 1081

Chocolate set consisting of chocolate pot, 10¼″ tall and six cups and saucers, blue mark #52

Plate 1082

Chocolate set consisting of chocolate pot which is 10″ tall and six cups and saucers, green mark #47

Plate 1083

Chocolate set consisting of chocolate pot which is 9½″ tall and four cups and saucers, green mark #81

Plate 1084

Chocolate pot, 9¾″ tall, blue mark #52

Plate 1085

Chocolate set, chocolate pot is 9″ tall, four cups and saucers, green mark #79

Plate 1086

Chocolate set, pot is 9½″ tall, four cups and saucers, blue mark #52

Plate 1087

After dinner coffee set, pot is 9″ tall, six cups and saucers, all pieces have heavy gold dragon motif, green mark #47

Plate 1088

Chocolate pot, 9¾″ tall, blue mark #52

Plate 1083

Plate 1084

Plate 1085

Plate 1086

Plate 1087

Plate 1088

Plate 1089

Plate 1090

Plate 1089

    After dinner coffee set, pot is 6½" tall, set includes four cups and saucers, copper saucers are incised
"NANNING QUALITY
BOWNAN
MERIDAN CONN. 163"
red mark #47

Plate 1090

    Three piece tea set, pot is 6½" tall, green mark #47

Plate 1091

    Chocolate set, pot is 10½" tall, six cups and saucers, green mark #47

Plate 1092

    Chocolate set, pot is 10" tall, four cups and saucers, blue mark #52

Plate 1091

Plate 1092

Plate 1093

Plate 1094

Plate 1093

      Chocolate pot, 9½″ tall, mark #47
      Chocolate pot 9¾″ tall, blue mark #38
      Chocolate pot, 8½″ tall, blue mark #52

Plate 1094

      After dinner coffee set, pot is 6½″ tall, five cups and saucers, green mark #81

Plate 1095

      After dinner coffee set, pot is 8″ tall, tray is 12″ wide, set also includes six cups and saucers, green mark #47

Plate 1096

      Chocolate set, pot is 9¾″ tall, four cups and saucers, green mark #52

Plate 1095

Plate 1096

Plate 1097

Plate 1098

Plate 1097

Tea set consisting of teapot, creamer, sugar and four cups and saucers, pot is 5″ tall, blue mark #52

Plate 1098

Tea set consisting of teapot, creamer, sugar and six cups and saucers, pot is 4″ tall, blue mark #52

Plate 1099

After dinner coffee set consisting of pot, five cups and saucers, and salt and pepper shakers, mark #109

Plate 1100

Chocolate set consisting of pot which is 9½″ tall and four cups and saucers, blue mark #84
Matching cake plate, 10½″ wide, blue mark #84
Matching cookie or cracker jar, 8″ wide, blue mark #84

Plate 1099

Plate 1100

209

Plate 1102

Plate 1101

Plate 1103

Plate 1101

    Three piece tea set, pot is 5½″ tall, blue mark #52

Plate 1102

    Chocolate pot, 12¼″ tall, blue mark #52

Plate 1103

    Tea set consisting of teapot, creamer, sugar and six cups and saucers, pot is 6½″ tall, mark #71

Plate 1104

    Tea set consisting of teapot, creamer, sugar, six cups and saucers, blue mark #52
    Matching 5″ covered milk pitcher, green mark #47
    Matching salt and pepper shakers, blue mark #52

Plate 1105

    Tea set consisting of teapot, creamer, sugar and four cups and saucers, green mark #47
    Matching 9″ vase, blue mark #52
    Matching salt and pepper shakers, unmarked

Plate 1104

Plate 1105

211

Plate 1106

Plate 1107

Plate 1108

Plate 1106

Tea set consisting of teapot, creamer and sugar and six cups and saucers, pot is 6½″ tall including finial, mark #71

Plate 1107

Tea set consisting of teapot, creamer and sugar and eight cups and saucers, pot is 5½″ tall, green mark #47

Plate 1108

Three piece tea set, pot is 5″ tall, mark #106

Plate 1109

Tea set consisting of teapot, creamer and sugar and six cups and saucers; pot is 5½″ tall, blue mark #52

Plate 1110

Tea set consisting of teapot, creamer and sugar and six cups and saucers, pot is 5¼″ tall, mark #73

Plate 1109

Plate 1110

213

Plate 1111

Plate 1112

Plate 1113

Plate 1111

Tea set consisting of teapot, creamer, sugar and six cups and saucers, pot is 5¼″ tall, blue mark #71

Plate 1112

Three piece tea set, pot is 6¾″ tall, sugar is 5″, creamer is 4½″, blue mark #32

Plate 1113

Cake plate, 11½″ wide including handles, green mark #52
Cake plate, 10″ wide, blue mark #52

Plate 1114

Chocolate pot, 10″ tall, blue mark #52

Plate 1115

Tea set consisting of teapot, creamer, sugar and six cups and saucers, pot is 6″ tall, green mark #47

Plate 1116

Chocolate pot, 10½″ tall, blue mark #52

Plate 1117

Three piece tea set, some moriage trim, pot is 4″ tall, green mark #47

Plate 1118

Cake set, large plate is 11″ in diameter, small plates are 6″, blue mark #52

Plate 1119

Cake set, large plate 10½″ in diameter, six small plates, each 5¾″ wide, mark #81

214

Plate 1114

Plate 1115

Plate 1116

Plate 1117

Plate 1118

Plate 1119

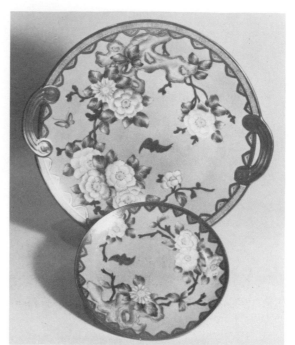

Plate 1120

Plate 1121

Plate 1120

Cake set, large plate 11″ wide plus six smaller plates, green mark #47

Plate 1121

Cake set, large plate 11″ wide plus six smaller plates, green mark #47

Plate 1122

Cake set, large plate 10½″ wide, plus six smaller plates, mark #87

Plate 1122

Plate 1123

Lemonade set consisting of pitcher which is 6¼″ tall and six cups, green mark #113

Plate 1124

Bowl, 9″ wide, green mark #47

Plate 1125

Peanut set, master bowl is 8½″ long, six smaller dishes are 3½″ long, green mark #47

Plate 1126

Five piece hostess set in lacquered box, blue mark #52

Plate 1127

Celery set consisting of 13½″ long celery dish and six salts 3¾″ long, green mark #47

Plate 1128

Large fruit compote, 12″ wide including handles, blue mark #52

Plate 1123

Plate 1124

Plate 1125

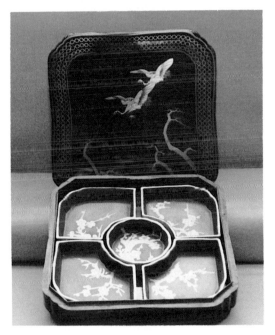

Plate 1126

Plate 1127

Plate 1128

Plate 1129

Plate 1130

Plate 1131

Plate 1132

Plate 1129

    Bowl set, large bowl is 9½″ wide, six smaller bowls are 5″ wide, blue mark #52

Plate 1130

    Nut set, large bowl is 8¾″ wide, four small bowls are 3¾″ wide, green mark #47

Plate 1131

    Nut set, large bowl is 7½″ wide, five smaller bowls are 3¼″ wide, green mark #52

Plate 1132

    Bowl, 11″ wide including handles, mark #89

Plate 1133

    Bowl, 8¼″ wide, green mark #47

Plate 1134

    Bowl, 6½″ wide, green mark #47

Plate 1135

    Nut set, large bowl is 7½″ wide, six smaller bowls are 3″ wide, green mark #47

Plate 1136

    Two piece fruit bowl on pedestal (could also be used as small punch bowl), 5¼″ tall, green mark #47

Plate 1137

    Nut set, large bowl is 7½″ wide, six smaller bowls are 3″ wide, green mark #47

Plate 1138

    Bowl, 8½″ diameter, green mark #47

Plate 1133

Plate 1134

Plate 1135

Plate 1136

Plate 1137

Plate 1138

Plate 1139

Plate 1140

Plate 1141

Plate 1142

Plate 1143

Plate 1139

    Bowl, 8½″ wide, green mark #47
    Bowl, 9″ wide, green mark #47

Plate 1140

    Bowl, 10½″ wide, mark #39

Plate 1141

    Bowl, 9″ wide, green mark #47

Plate 1142

    Bowl, 7½″ wide, green mark #47

Plate 1143

    Bowl, 8″ wide, green mark #47

Plate 1144

    Bowl, 9″ wide, green mark #47

Plate 1145

    Pair of candlesticks, 9½″ tall, blue mark #52

Plate 1146

    Pair of candlesticks, 8½″ tall, green mark #47

Plate 1147

    Pair of candlesticks, 8¼″ tall, green mark #47
    Matching ashtray, 4¾″ long, green mark #47

Plate 1148

    Pair of candlesticks, 6¼″ tall, green mark #47

Plate 1149

    Candlestick, 6¼″ tall, green mark #47
    Candlestick, 6¼″ tall, same mold, different decoration, green mark #47

Plate 1144

Plate 1145

Plate 1146

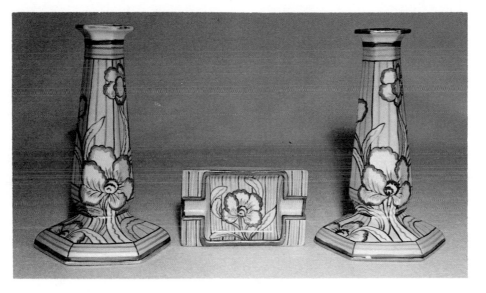

Plate 1147

Plate 1148

Plate 1149

Plate 1150

Plate 1151

Plate 1152

Plate 1153

Plate 1150

Bowl, 10½″ in diameter, blue mark #52

Plate 1151

Nut set, large bowl is on pedestal and is 7½″ in diameter, six small cups, green mark #47

Plate 1152

Bowl, 8½″ wide, green mark #47

Plate 1153

Pair of candlesticks, 8½″ tall, green mark #47
Ferner, 6″ long, green mark #47

Plate 1154

Candlestick, 8¼″ tall, blue mark #47

Plate 1155

Dresser set consisting of tray which is 11″ long, hatpin holder, 5″ tall, pin dish which is 5″ wide, hair receiver, 3″ tall and perfume bottle, 5″ tall, green mark #47

Plate 1156

Vanity organizer which is a combination stickpin holder, hatpin holder and ring tree, tray is 7″ long, blue mark #52
Hanging wall vase, 7″ long, blue mark #52

Plate 1157

Candlestick, 8″ tall, blue mark #47

Plate 1158

Heart shaped trinket box, 4″ wide, blue mark #52
Ring holder, 3½″ tall, blue mark #52

Plate 1159

Dresser set, tray is 11″ long, hatpin is 4½″ tall, green mark #47

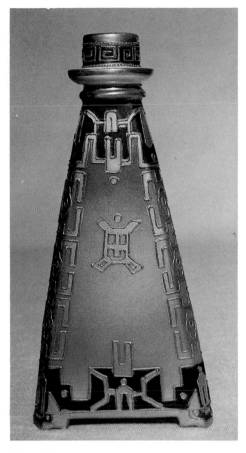

Plate 1154

Plate 1155

Plate 1156

Plate 1157

Plate 1158

Plate 1159

223

Plate 1160

Plate 1161

Plate 1162

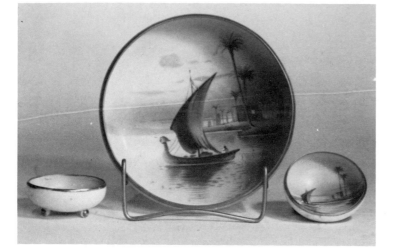

Plate 1163

Plate 1164

Plate 1160

Nut bowl, 7½″ wide, green mark #47

Plate 1161

Powder box, 4″ wide, green mark #47

Plate 1162

Talcum powder flask, 5″ tall, blue mark #68

Plate 1163

Nut set, large bowl 7¼″ in diameter, six small cups, 3″ in diameter, green mark #47

Plate 1164

Hairpin holder, 3″ tall, green mark #47

Plate 1165

Bowl, 6″ wide, green mark #47

Plate 1166

Dresser set, tray is 11″ long, mark #103

Plate 1167

Hatpin holders, all open top
1. 4¾″ tall, mark #68
2. 4¾″ tall, blue mark #52
3. 4¾″ tall, mark #7
4. 4⅞″ tall, mark #84
5. 4⅞″ tall, blue mark # 52

Plate 1168

Hatpin holders
1. 4¾″ tall, green mark #47
2. 4¾″ tall, mark #84
3. 4¾″ tall, green mark #47
4. 4¾″ tall, red mark #47
5. 4¾″ tall, mark #103

Plate 1169

Bowl, 6″ wide, green mark #47

Plate 1170

Hatpin holders
1. 4¾″ tall, holes in top, blue mark #47
2. 4⅝″ tall, open top, green mark #47
3. 4¾″ tall, open top, green mark #47
4. 4⅝″ tall, open top, green mark #47
5. 4¾″ tall, open top, green mark #47

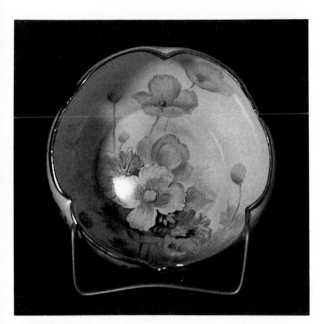

Plate 1165

Plate 1166

Plate 1167

Plate 1168

Plate 1169

Plate 1170

Plate 1171

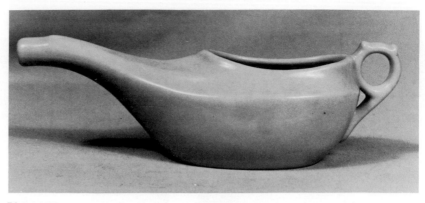

Plate 1172

Plate 1173

Plate 1174

Plate 1175

Plate 1171

Cruet, 7¼″ tall, green mark #47

Plate 1172

Feeding boat, 8″ long, 2½″ tall, mark #55

Plate 1173

Two piece butter dish, bottom plate is 7¾″ in diameter, green mark #47

Plate 1174

Double sugar cube holder, 5¾″ long including handles, green mark #47

Plate 1175

Sugar shaker, 4¾″ tall, mark #17
Sugar shaker, 3½″ tall, green mark #47

Plate 1176

Sugar shaker, 5″ tall, green mark #47
Sugar shaker, 5″ tall, blue mark #52
Sugar shaker, 5″ tall, green mark #47

Plate 1177

Syrup with underplate, 6″ tall, green mark #52

Plate 1178

Egg warmer, 5½″ in diameter, green mark #47
Sugar shaker, 5″ tall, blue mark #52

Plate 1179

Double egg cup, 3½″ tall, mark #93
Single egg cup, 2½″ tall, mark #93

Plate 1180

Egg server, 6¼″ wide, blue mark #84

Plate 1181

Tea tiles, each 5½″ wide, green mark #47

Plate 1176

Plate 1177

Plate 1178

Plate 1179

Plate 1181

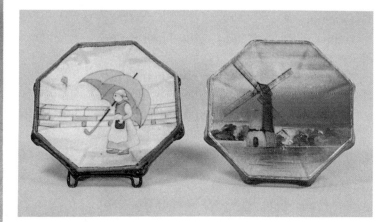

Plate 1180

Plate 1182

Plate 1183

Plate 1184

Plate 1185

Plate 1186

Plate 1182

    Creamer and sugar, sugar is 7″ wide and creamer is 6½″ wide, blue mark #39

Plate 1183

    Tea strainer, 6″ long, unmarked

Plate 1184

    Tea strainer, 6″ long, blue mark #52

    Tea strainer, 6″ long, blue mark #52

Plate 1185

    Individual tea pot, 4¾″ tall, blue mark #4

Plate 1186

    Sugar and creamer and matching tray, tray is 8¾″ long, sugar is 3½″ tall and creamer is 2½″ tall, green mark #47

Plate 1187

    Condensed milk holder with underplate, 6″ tall, mark #80

    Condensed milk holder with underplate, 6″ tall, green mark #47

Plate 1188

    Basket dish, 7″ long, green mark #47

Plate 1189

    Toast rack, 8¼″ long, blue mark #84

Plate 1190

    Creamer, sugar and two piece butter dish, butter dish is 7½″ in diameter, sugar is 4¾″ tall, blue mark #52

Plate 1191

    Shaving mug, 4″ tall, green mark #47

Plate 1192

    Serving dish, 8″ wide, blue mark #84

Plate 1193

    Mustache cup, blue mark #52

    Mustache cup, green mark #47

Plate 1194

    Bon bon dish, 5½″ wide, green mark #47

Plate 1187

Plate 1188

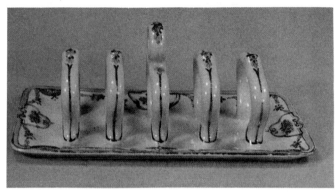

Plate 1189

Plate 1190

Plate 1191

Plate 1192

Plate 1193

Plate 1194

229

Plate 1195

Plate 1196

Plate 1197

Plate 1198

Plate 1199

Plate 1195

　　Lamp, 12½″ tall, mark unknown.

Plate 1196

　　Flower arranger, 5½″ wide, 3½″ tall, blue mark #52

Plate 1197

　　Knife rest, 3½″ long, green mark #47

Plate 1198

　　Punch cups, each 2¾″ tall, green mark #47

Plate 1199

　　Toothpick holder, 2″ tall, green mark #47

Plate 1200

　　Set of 8 luncheon plates, each 9″ wide, blue mark #52

Plate 1201

　　Covered jar, 6¼″ tall, unmarked
　　Cup, 2½″ tall, green mark #52
　　Syrup and underplate, 6½″ tall, green mark #52
　　Mug, 4½″ tall, green mark #52

Plate 1202

　　Potpourri jar, 5¾″ tall, green mark #47

Plate 1203

　　Toothpick holder, 2¼″ tall, green mark #47
　　Toothpick holder, 2″ tall, blue mark #52
　　Toothpick holder, 2¾″ tall, green mark #47
　　Toothpick holder, 2¼″ tall, blue mark #84
　　Toothpick holder, 2½″ tall, green mark #47

Plate 1204

　　Sauce dish, underplate and ladle, underplate is 5½″ long, green mark #47

Plate 1205

　　Bell shaped match holder and striker, 3½″ tall, green mark #47
　　Bell shaped match holder and striker, 3½″ tall, mark #82
　　also has original sticker #53

Plate 1206

230　　Two tier dish, bottom measures 6″, top is 3″ wide, blue mark #84

Plate 1200

Plate 1201

Plate 1203

Plate 1205

Plate 1202

Plate 1204

Plate 1206

231

Plate 1207

Plate 1208

Plate 1210

Plate 1209

Plate 1207
     Ginger jar, 7½″ tall, mark #55
Plate 1208
     Mayonnaise set with underplate and ladle, 7″ wide, blue mark #52
Plate 1209
     Milk pitcher, 7″ tall, green mark #47
Plate 1210
     Slanted cheese dish, 7½″ long, green mark #47
     Condiment dish, 5¼″ tall, green mark #47

INDEX TO PHOTOS OF SOME OF THE UNIQUE PATTERNS, TECHNIQUES AND TEXTURES FOUND ON NIPPON ITEMS

INDEX TO NIPPON ITEMS PHOTOGRAPHED IN BOOK

BIBLIOGRAPHY

Angione, Genevieve, *"All-Bisque And Half Bisque Dolls"*, Thomas Nelson, Inc., Nashville & N.Y. 1969

Angione, Genevieve & Whorton, Judith, *"All Dolls Are Collectible"*, Everybodys Press Inc., Hanover, Pa. 1977

Coleman, Dorothy S., Elizabeth A. & Evelyn J., *"The Collectors Encyclopedia of Dolls"*, Crown Publishers Inc., NY 1968

Marion, Frieda & Werner, Norma *"The Collector's Encyclopedia of Half-Dolls,"* Collector Books, Paducah, Ky. 1979

Miller, Robert, W., *"Wallace-Homestead Price Guide to Dolls"*, Wallace-Homestead, Des Moines, Iowa 1975

Punchard, Lorraine, M., *"Playtime Dishes"*, Wallace-Homestead Book Co., Des Moines, Iowa 1978

Smith, Patricia, R., *"Antique Collector Dolls"*, Collector Books, Paducah, Ky. 1975
 "Antique Collector Dolls", Second Series, Collector Books, Paducah, Ky. 1976
 "Oriental Dolls", Collector Books, Paducah, Ky. 1979

Tanaka, Seno, *"The Tea Ceremony"*, Harmony Books, NYC 1973

Glossary

American Indian design – a popular collectible in Nippon porcelain, these designs include the Indian in a canoe, Indian warrior, Indian hunting wild game and the Indian maiden.

Apricot (ume) – in Japan, stands for strength and nobility, is also a symbol of good luck.

Art Deco – a style of decoration which hit its peak in Europe and America around 1925 although items were manufactured with this decor as early as 1910. The style was modernistic. Geometric patterns were popular. Motifs used were shapes such as circles, rectangles, cylinders and cones.

Art Nouveau – the name is derived from the French words meaning new art. During the period of 1885-1925, artists tended to use bolder colors and realism was rejected. Free flowing designs were used, breaking away from the limitations of the past.

Artist signed – items signed by the artist, most appear to be of English extraction probably painted during the heyday of hand painting chinaware at the turn of the century.

Azalea pattern – pattern found on Nippon items, pink azaleas with green to gray leaves and gold rims. Nippon marked pieces match the Noritake marked azalea pattern items. The Azalea pattern was originally offered by the Larkin Co. to its customers as premiums.

Backstamp – mark found on Nippon porcelain items identifying the manufacturer, exporter or importer and country of origin.

Bamboo tree – symbolic of strength, faithfulness and honesty in Japan, also a good luck symbol. The bamboo resists the storm but it yields to it and rises again.

Beading – generally a series of clay dots applied on Nippon porcelain, very often enameled over in gold. Later Nippon pieces merely had dots of enameling.

Blank – greenware of bisque items devoid of decoration.

Blown-out items – this term is used by collectors and dealers for items that have a molded relief pattern embossed by the mold in which the article was shaped. It is not actually "blown-out" as glass items are, but the pattern is raised from the background of the item. (See Molded Relief)

Biscuit – clay which has been fired but unglazed.

Bisque – same as biscuit, term also used by collectors to describe a matte finish on an item.

Böttger, Johanne, F. – a young German alchemist who supposedly discovered the value of kaolin in making porcelain. This discovery helped to revolutionize the china-making industry in Europe beginning in the early 1700's.

Carp – fish that symbolizes strength and perseverance.

Casting – the process of making reproductions by pouring slip into molds.

Cha no yu – Japanese tea ceremony.

Chargers – archaic term for large platters or plates.

Cheese hard clay – same as leather hard clay.

Cherry blossoms – national flower of Japan and emblem of the faithful warrior.

Ching-tê-Chên – ancient city in China where nearly a million people lived and worked with almost all devoted to the making of porcelain.

Chrysanthemum – depicts health and longevity, the crest of the Emperor of Japan. The chrysanthemum blooms late in the year and lives longer than other flowers.

Citron – stands for wealth.

Cloisonne on Porcelain – on Nippon porcelain wares it resembles the other cloisonne pieces except that it was produced on a porcelain body instead of metal. The decoration is divided into cells called cloisons. The cloisons are divided by strips of metal wire which kept the colors separated during the firing.

Cobalt oxide – blue oxide imported to Japan after 1868 for decoration of wares. Gosu, a pebble found in Oriental riverbeds had previously been used but was scarce and more expensive than the imported oxide. Cobalt oxide is the most powerful of all the coloring oxides for tinting.

Coralene items – were made by firing small colored beads on the wares. Most are signed Kinran, US Patent, NBR 912171, February 9, 1909, Japan. Tiny glass beads had previously been applied to glass items in the shapes of birds, flowers, leaves, etc. and no doubt this was an attempt to copy it. Japanese coralene was patented by Alban L. Rock, an American living in Yokohama, Japan. The virtreous coating of beads gave the item a plush velvety look. The beads were permanently fired on and gave a luminescence to the design. The most popular design had been one of seaweed and coral hence the name *coralene* was given to this type of design.

Crane – a symbol of good luck in Japan, also stands for marital fidelity and is an emblem of longevity.

Daffodil – a sign of spring to the Japanese.

Decalcomania – a process of transferring a wet paper print onto the surface of an item. It was made to resemble hand painted work.

Deer – stands for divine messenger.

Diaper pattern – repetitive pattern of small design used on Nippon porcelain, often geometric or floral.

Dragons (ryu) – a symbol of strength, goodness and good fortune. The Japanese dragon has three claws and was thought to reside in the sky. Clouds, water and lightening often accompany the dragon. The dragon is often portrayed in high relief using the slip trailing method of decor.

Drain mold – a mold used in making hollow ware. Liquid slip is poured into the mold until the desired thickness of the walls is achieved. The excess clay is poured out.

Drape mold – or flopover mold, used to make flat bottomed items. Moist clay is rolled out and draped over the mold. It is then pressed firmly into shape.

Dutch scenes – popular on Nippon items, include those of windmills, and men and women dressed in Dutch costumes.

Edo – or Yedo, the largest city in Japan, later renamed Tokyo, meaning eastern capitol.

Embossed design – see molded relief.

Enamel beading – dots of enameling painted by the artist in gold or other colors and often made to resemble jewels such as emeralds and rubies. Many times this raised beading will be found in brown or black colors.

Fairings – items won or bought at fairs as a souvenir of the event.

Feldspar – most common rock found on earth.

Fern leaves – symbolic of ample good fortune.

Fettles or mold marks – ridges formed where sections of molds are joined at the seam. These fettles have to be removed before the item is decorated.

Finial – the top knob on a cover of an item, used to lift the cover off.

Firing – the cooking or baking of clay ware.

Flopover mold – same as a drape mold.

Flux – an ingredient added to glaze to assist in making the item fire properly. It causes the glaze to melt at a specified temperature.

Glaze – composed of silica, alumina and flux, and is applied to porcelain pieces. During the firing process the glaze joins together with the clay item to form a glasslike surface. It seals the pores and makes the item impervious to liquids.

Gold trim – has to be fired at lower temperatures or the gold would sink into the enameled decoration. If overfired, the gold becomes discolored.

Gouda ceramics – originally made in Gouda, a province of South Holland. These items were copied on the Nippon wares and were patterned after the Art Nouveau style.

Gosu – pebble found in Oriental riverbeds, a natural cobalt. It was used to color items until 1868 when oxidized cobalt was introduced into Japan.

Greenware – clay which has been molded but not fired.

Hard paste porcelain – paste meaning the body of substance, porcelain being made from clay using kaolin. This produces a hard translucent body when fired.

Ho-o bird – sort of a bird of paradise who resides on earth and is associated with the Empress of Japan. Also see phoenix bird.

Incised backstamp – the backstamp marking is scratched into the surface of a clay item.

Incised decoration – a sharp tool or stick was used to produce the design right onto the body of the article while it was still in a state of soft clay.

Iris – the Japanese believe this flower wards off evil, it is associated with warriors because of its sword-like leaves.

Jasper Ware – see Wedgwood.

Jigger – a machine resembling a potter's wheel. Soft pliable clay is placed onto a convex revolving mold. As the wheel turns, a template is held against it trimming off the excess clay on the outside. The revolving mold shapes the inside of the item and the template cuts the outside.

Jolley – a machine like a jigger only in reverse. The revolving mold is concave and the template forms the inside of the item. The template is lowered inside the revolving mold. The mold forms the outside surface while the template cuts the inside.

Jomon – neolithic hunters and fishermen in Japan dating back to approximately 2500 B.C. Their pottery was hand formed and marked with an overall rope or cord pattern. It was made of unwashed clay, unglazed and was baked in open fires.

Kaga – province in Japan.

Kaolin – a highly refractory clay and one of the principal ingredients used in making porcelain. It is a pure white residual clay, a decomposition of granite.

Kao-ling – a word meaning "the high hills" in Chinese, the word kaolin is derived from it.

Kiln – oven in which pottery is fired.

Leather hard clay – clay which is dry enough to hold its shape but still damp and moist, no longer in a plastic state, also called cheese hard.

Liquid slip – clay in a liquid state.

Lobster – symbol of long life.

Luster decoration – a metallic type of coloring decoration, gives an iridescent effect.

Matte finish – also referred to as mat and matt. A dull glaze having a low reflectance when fired.

McKinley Tariff Act of 1890 – Chapter 1244, Section 6 states "That on and after the first day of March, eighteen hundred and ninety-one, all articles of foreign manufacture, such as are usually or ordinarily marked, stamped, branded or labeled, and all packages containing such or other imported articles, shall, respectively, be plainly marked, stamped, branded or labeled in legible English words, so as to indicate the country of their origin; and unless so marked, stamped, branded, or labeled they shall not be admitted to entry."

Meiji period – period of 1868-1912 in Japan when Emperor Mutsuhito reigned. It means enlightened rule.

Middle East scenes – popular design used on Nippon pieces. They feature pyramids, deserts, palm trees and riders on camels.

Model – the shape from which the mold is made.

Molded relief items – the pattern is embossed on the item by the mold in which the article is shaped. These items give the appearance that the pattern is caused by some type of upward pressure from the underside. Collectors often refer to these items as "blown-out."

Molds – contain a cavity in which castings are made. They are generally made from plaster of paris and are used for shaping clay objects. Both liquid and plastic clay may be used. The mold can also be made of clay or rubber, however, plaster was generally used as it absorbs moisture immediately from the clay. Raised ornamentation may also be formed directly in the mold.

Moriage – refers to applied clay (slip) relief decoration. On Nippon items, this was usually done by "slip trailing" or hand rolling and shaping the clay on an item.

Morimura Bros. – importers of Japanese wares in the United Stastes and the sole importers of Noritake wares. It was opened in New York City in 1876 and closed in 1941.

Mutsuhito – Emperor of Japan from 1868-1912. His reign was called the Meiji period which meant enlightened rule.

Nagoya – a large city in Japan.

Narcissus – stands for good fortune.

Ningyo – Japanese name for doll, meaning human being and image.

Nippon – the name the Japanese people called their country. It comes from a Chinese phrase maning "the source of the sun" and sounds like Neehon in Japanese.

Noritake Co. – originally registered as Nippon Gomei Kaisha. In 1917 the name was change to Nippon Toki Kabushiki Toki. From 1918 the word Noritake appeared in conjunction with Nippon which was the designation of country of origin.

Orchid – means hidden beauty and modesty to the Japanese.

Overglaze decoration – a design is either painted or a decal applied to an item which already has a fired glazed surface. The article is then refired to make the decoration permanent.

Pattern stamping – the design was achieved by using a special stamp or a plaster roll having the design cut into it. The design was pressed into the soft clay body of an item.

Panch – drink originating in India consisting of lemon juice, arrack, tea, sugar and water.

Paulownia flower – crest of the Empress of Japan.

Peach – stands for marriage.

Peacock – stands for elegance and beauty.

Peony – considered the king of flowers in Japan.

Perry, Matthew, Comm., USN – helped to fashion the Kanagawa treaty in 1854 between the United States and Japan. This treaty opened the small ports of Shimoda and Hakodate to trade. Shipwrecked sailors were also to receive good treatment and an American Consul was permitted to reside at Shimoda.

Petuntse – clay found in felspathic rocks such as granite. Its addition to porcelain made the item more durable. Petuntse is also called china stone.

Phoenix bird – sort of a bird of paradise which resides on earth and is associated with the Empress of Japan. This bird appears to be a cross between a peacock, a pheasant and gamecock. There appear to be many designs for this bird as each artist had his own conception as to how it should look. It is also a symbol to the Japanese of all that is beautiful.

Pickard Co. – a china decorating studio originally located in Chicago. This firm decorated blank wares imported from a number of countries including Nippon.

Pine tree – to the Japanese this tree is symbolic of friendship and prosperity and depicts the winter season. It is also a sign of good luck and a sign of strength.

Plastic clay – clay in a malleable state, able to be shaped and formed without collapsing.

Plum – stands for womanhood. Plum blossoms reflect bravery.

Porcelain – a mixture composed mainly of kaolin and petuntse which are fired at a high temperature and vitrified.

Porcelain slip – porcelain clay in a liquid form.

Porcellaine – French adaption of the word porcelain.

Porcellana – Italian word meaning cowry shell. The Chinese ware which was brought back to Venice in the 15th century was thought to resemble the cowry shell and was called porcellana.

Portrait items – items decorated with portraits, many of Victorian ladies. Some appear to be hand painted, others are decal work.

Potter's wheel – rotating device onto which a ball of plastic clay is placed. The wheel is turned and the potter molds the clay with his hands and is capable of producing cylindrical objects.

Pottery – on its broadest sense includes all forms of wares made from clay.

Press mold – used to make handles, finials, figurines, etc. A two-piece mold into which soft clay is placed. The two pieces are pressed together to form items.

Relief – molded (see Molded Relief Items).

Royal Ceramics – name of Nippon pieces marked with RC on backstamp.

Satsuma – a sea-going principality in Japan, an area where many of the old famous kilns are found, and also a type of Japanese ware. Satsuma is a cream-colored glazed pottery which is finely crackled.

Slip – liquid clay.

Slip trailing – a process where liquid clay was applied to porcelain via a bamboo or rubber tube. A form of painting but with clay instead of paint. The slip is often applied quite heavily and gives a thick, raised appearance.

Slurry – thick slip.

Solid casting mold – used for shallow type items such as bowls and plates. In this type of mold, the thickness of the walls is determined by the mold and ever piece is formed identical. The mold shapes both the inside and the outside of the piece and the thickness of the walls can be controlled. Solid casting can be done with either liquid or plastic clay.

Sometsuke style decoration – items decorated with an underglaze of blue and white colors.

Sprigging – the application of small molded relief decoration to the surface of porcelain by use of liquid clay as in Jasper Ware.

Sprig mold – a one-piece mold used in making ornaments. Clay is fitted or poured onto a mold which is incised with a design. Only one side is molded and the exposed side becomes the back of the finished item.

Taisho – name of the period reigned over by Emperor Yoshihito in Japan from 1912-1926. It means great peace.

Tapestry – a type of decor used on Nippon porcelain. A cloth was dipped into liquid slip and then stretched onto the porcelain item. During the bisque firing the material burned off and left a textured look on the porcelain piece resembling needlepoint in many cases. The item was then painted and fired again in the usual manner.

Template – profile of the pattern being cut.

Throwing – the art of forming a clay object on a potter's wheel.

Tiger (tora) – a symbol of longevity.

Transfer print – see Decalcomania.

Translucent – not transparent but clear enough to allow rays of light to pass through.

Ultra violet lamp – lamp used to detect cracks and hidden repairs in items.

Underglaze decoration – this type of decoration is applied on bisque china (fired once), then the item is glazed and fired again.

Victorian Age design – decor used on some Nippon pieces, gaudy and extremely bold colors used.

Vitreous – glass-like.

Vitrify – to change into a glass-like substance due to the application of heat.

Wasters – a word for pieces ruined or marred in the kiln.

Water lilies – represents autumn in Japan.

Wedgwood – term used to refer to Nippon pieces which attempt to imitate Josiah Wedgwood's Jasper Ware. The items generally have a light blue or green background. The Nippon pieces were produced with a slip trailing decor, however, rather than the sprigging ornamentation made popular by Wedgwood. White clay slip was trailed onto the background color of the item by use of tubing to form the pattern.

Yamato – district in central Japan.

Yayoi – people of the bronze and iron culture in Japan dating back to 300-100 B.C. They were basically an agriculture people. They made pottery using the potter's wheel.

Yedo – or Edo, the largest city in Japan, renamed Tokyo meaning eastern capitol.

Yoshihito – Emperor of Japan from 1912-1926. He took the name of Taisho which meant great peace.

Series II

In this guide, you will find an estimated RETAIL price listed for each item photographed. Price quotes are for similar pieces in MINT condition. Adjustments in price should be made for cracks, chips, worn gold, repairs, etc.

At their best, most of these prices will be controversial. However, collectors and dealers should realize that they are just that—a guide. They are a starting point in determining a price and are not intended to set them.

Buy pieces that you like and also buy quality. This is a winning combination and no matter what the fickle market does, you will still have a collection with which you will be happy.

PAGES 50 and 51

Plate 367
    Cobalt scenic vase, 9½" T., blue mark #52 .... $550.00 – 650.00
Plate 368
    Cobalt scenic vase, 9½" T., blue mark #52 .... $550.00 – 650.00
Plate 369
    Cobalt scenic cracker or cookie jar, 8½" T., blue mark #52 .. $550.00 – 625.00
Plate 370
    Cobalt scenic vase, 7" T., blue mark #52 .... $425.00 – 500.00
Plate 371
    Cobalt scenic urn, 17" T., blue mark #52 .... $3,000.00 – 3,600.00
Plate 372
    Cobalt scenic bowls, 7" dia., blue mark #52.............(Each) $275.00 – 350.00
    Cobalt scenic vase, 10½" T., blue mark #52 .... $600.00 – 700.00

PAGES 52 and 53

Plate 373
    Cobalt scenic cookie or cracker jar, 8½" T., blue mark#52 $500.00 – 575.00
Plate 374
    Cobalt scenic tea set, set has teapot 5½" T., creamer,
    sugar and six cups and saucers, blue mark #52 .... $1,000.00 – 1,200.00
Plate 375
    Cobalt and gold vase, 12½" T., blue mark #52 .... $600.00 – 700.00
Plate 376
    Cobalt scenic cake set, large plate 10¾" W., six small
    plates 6¼" W., blue mark #52 .... $550.00 – 650.00
Plate 377
    Cobalt and floral pitcher, 7" T., blue mark #52 .... $450.00 – 525.00
Plate 378
    Cobalt and gold vase, 6½" T., blue mark #52 .... $325.00 – 375.00
    Cobalt scenic vase, 6½" T., blue mark #52 .... $400.00 – 475.00
Plate 379
    Cobalt scenic covered jar 5" T., blue mark #52 .... $250.00 – 300.00
    Cobalt scenic pitcher, 6¾" T., blue mark #52 .... $250.00 – 300.00

PAGES 54 and 55

Plate 380
    Cobalt scenic plate, 8¾" W., blue mark #47 .... $300.00 – 375.00
    Cobalt scenic plate, 8½" W., green mark #47 .... $250.00 – 300.00
Plate 381
    Cobalt and floral pitcher, 7½" T., blue mark #52 .... $450.00 – 525.00
Plate 382
    Cobalt and floral vase, 14¼" T., blue mark #52 .... $600.00 – 700.00
Plate 383
    Cobalt scenic cake plate, 10¾" W., green mark #47 .... $275.00 – 350.00
Plate 384
    Cobalt scenic vase, 9½" T., blue mark #52 .... $425.00 – 500.00
    Cobalt scenic vase, 9" T., blue mark #52 .... $350.00 – 425.00
Plate 385
    Cobalt and floral plate, 8" W., blue mark #52 .... $300.00 – 375.00
Plate 386
    Cobalt and floral pitcher, 5¾" T., green mark #52 .... $400.00 – 475.00

PAGES 56 and 57

Plate 387
    Cobalt and gold plate, 8½" W., green mark #47 .... $100.00 – 150.00
Plate 388
    Cobalt and floral plates, 7½" W., blue mark #52 ....(Each) $75.00 – 100.00
Plate 389
    Cobalt scenic covered urn, 13¾" T., blue mark #114 .... $1,500.00 – 1,800.00

Plate 390
    Cobalt ewer, w/heavy gold overlay, 10" T., blue mark #52 .. $625.00 – 725.00
Plate 391
    Cobalt scenic vase, 13" T., green mark #47 .... $525.00 – 600.00
Plate 392
    Cobalt & heavy gold overlay humidor, 7½" T., blue mark #52 .. $750.00 – 850.00

PAGES 58 and 59

Plate 393
    Cobalt scenic vase, 13" T., blue mark #52 .... $500.00 – 600.00
Plate 394
    Cobalt and gold chocolate set, pot 9½" T., blue mark #52;
    four cups and saucers; matching 12" dia. tray, blue mark
    #71 .... $1,000.00 – 1,200.00
Plate 395
    Cobalt scenic tankard, 10¼" T., blue mark #47 .... $600.00 – 700.00
Plate 396
    Cobalt scenic vase, 14" T., blue mark #52 .... $600.00 – 700.00
Plate 397
    Cobalt scenic vase, 9" T., green mark #47 .... $350.00 – 450.00
    Cobalt scenic vase, 9½" T., green mark #47 .... $325.00 – 400.00
Plate 398
    Cobalt scenic vase, 12" T., green mark #47 .... $425.00 – 500.00

PAGES 60 and 61

Plate 399
    Demitasse cups and saucers, cobalt and gold, cups 2"
    T., green mark #47 ....(Each) $50.00 – 75.00
Plate 400
    Tea set, cobalt & floral, pot 4½" T. (see Plate 401 for match-
    ing cups and saucers), blue mark #52 (Complete Set)...... $950.00 – 1,150.00
Plate 401
    Cups and saucers, cobalt and floral, matching Plate 400,
    blue mark #52 ....(Complete Set) $950.00 – 1,150.00
Plate 402
    Tea set, cobalt and gold, pot 5½" T., set has creamer,
    sugar, and eight cups and saucers, blue mark #71 .... $750.00 – 900.00

PAGES 62 and 63

Plate 403
    Tapestry bottle shaped vase, 8½" T., blue mark #52 .... $650.00 – 750.00
Plate 404
    Tapestry vase, 9½" T., blue mark #52 .... $650.00 – 750.00
Plate 405
    Tapestry vase, 6" T., blue mark #52 .... $525.00 – 600.00
Plate 406
    Tapestry vase, 5¼" T., blue mark #52 .... $550.00 – 650.00
    Tapestry vase, 8" T., blue mark #52 .... $650.00 – 750.00
    Tapestry vase, 5¼" T., blue mark #52 .... $550.00 – 650.00
Plate 407
    Tapestry covered urn, 10½" T., blue mark #52 .... $1,050.00 – 1,200.00
Plate 408
    Tapestry vase, 8½" T., blue mark #52 .... $1,100.00 – 1,300.00
Plate 409
    Tapestry ewer, 10¾" T., blue mark #52 .... $1,000.00 – 1,200.00

PAGES 64 and 65

Plate 410
    Tapestry vase, 8" T., blue mark #52 .... $450.00 – 525.00

Plate 411
Tapestry vase, 8" T., blue mark #52 .... $525.00 – 650.00
Plate 412
Tapestry vase, 9¼" T., blue mark #52 .... $600.00 – 700.00
Tapestry basket vase, 8¾" T., blue mark #52 .... $1,000.00 – 1,200.00
Plate 413
Tapestry vase, 6" T., blue mark #52 .... $500.00 – 600.00
Plate 414
Tapestry tankard, 10¾" T., blue mark #52 .... $850.00 – 1,000.00
Plate 415
Tapestry charger, 11¾" W., blue mark #52 .... $1,100.00 – 1,300.00
Plate 416
Tapestry ewer, 7" T., English hunt scene and Greek key
border, blue mark #52.. $800.00 – 950.00

PAGES 66 and 67

Plate 417
Wedgwood vase, 7½" T., green mark #47 .... $500.00 – 575.00
Plate 418
Wedgwood potpourri jar, 5½" T., green mark #47 .... $400.00 – 475.00
Plate 419
Wedgwood cup and saucer, green mark #47 .... $125.00 – 160.00
Plate 420
Wedgwood trimmed creamer and sugar, sugar 5" T. incl.
finial, green mark #47 .... $225.00 – 275.00
Plate 421
Wedgwood ferner, w/relief molded handles, 8½" W. incl.
handles, green mark #47 .... $550.00 – 700.00
Plate 422
Wedgwood vase, 8¾" T., green mark #47 .... $950.00 – 1,150.00
Wedgwood candlesticks, 6" T., green mark #47 ......(Pair) $475.00 – 575.00
Plate 423
Wedgwood trimmed vase, 9" T., green mark #47............. $400.00 – 500.00
Plate 424
Wedgwood candlesticks, 7½" T., green mark #47 ....(Pair) $550.00 – 650.00
Plate 425
Wedgwood vase, 8¼" T., green mark #47 .... $400.00 – 475.00
Plate 426
Wedgwood bowl, rare lavender color, 9¼" L., green mark #47 $275.00 – 350.00
Plate 427
Wedgwood slanted cheese dish, 7¾" L., green mark #47 $375.00 – 450.00
Plate 428
Wedgwood trimmed butter dish w/insert, 6" W., 3¾" T.,
green mark #47... $250.00 – 300.00

PAGES 68 and 69

Plate 429
Wedgwood trimmed scenic vase, 11" T., green mark #47 $450.00 – 550.00
Plate 430
Wedgwood trimmed floral vase, 8¾" T., rare lavender col-
or, green mark #47 .... $475.00 – 575.00
Plate 431
Wedgwood column ferner, 5" T., green mark #47 .... $450.00 – 550.00
Plate 432
Wedgwood trimmed floral relish dish, 7½" L., green mark
#47 .... $200.00 – 275.00
Plate 433
Wedgwood ashtray, 3" T., green mark #47 .... $300.00 – 375.00
Plate 434
Wedgwood cup and saucer, blue mark #8 .... $125.00 – 175.00
Plate 435
Wedgwood trimmed floral vase, 16" T., green mark #47 .. $900.00 – 1,100.00
Plate 436
Wedgwood ferner, 7" W., 3½" T., green mark #47 .... $400.00 – 475.00
Plate 437
Wedgwood vase, 9½" T., green mark #47 .... $475.00 – 550.00
Plate 438
Wedgwood trimmed floral bowl, 8¾" W. incl. handles,
green mark #47... $225.00 – 300.00
Wedgwood trimmed two-compartment relish dish, 8½"
W., green mark #47 .... $225.00 – 300.00

PAGES 70 and 71

Plate 439
Portrait vase 12" T., blue mark #52 .... $850.00 – 1,000.00

Plate 440
Portrait vase, 7" T., blue mark #52 .... $650.00 – 800.00
Plate 441
Portrait urn, 12" T., blue mark #52 .... $1,200.00 – 1,500.00
Plate 442
Portrait vases, 10" T., blue mark #52 ....(Each) $1,000.00 – 1,300.00
Plate 443
Portrait vase, 12" T., blue mark #52 .... $1,300.00 – 1,600.00
Plate 444
Portrait humidor, 7¾" T., blue mark #52 .... $1,000.00 – 1,200.00
Plate 445
Portrait dresser tray, 12" L., blue mark #52 .... $450.00 – 600.00

PAGES 72 and 73

Plate 446
Portrait vase, 9½" T., blue mark #52 .... $700.00 – 850.00
Plate 447
Portrait covered urn, 9½" T., blue mark #52 .... $850.00 – 1,000.00
Plate 448
Portrait mug, 5½" T., green mark #47 .... $400.00 – 500.00
Plate 449
Portrait plaque, 10" dia., green mark #42 .... $600.00 – 700.00
Plate 450
Portrait plaque, 10" dia., green mark #52 .... $600.00 – 700.00
Plate 451
Portrait vase, 9½" T., blue mark #52 .... $750.00 – 900.00
Plate 452
Portrait vase, 9" T., some moriage trim, blue mark #52 .... $600.00 – 700.00
Plate 453
Portrait stein, 7" T., green mark #47 .... $650.00 – 750.00
Plate 454
Portrait vase, 12" T., blue mark #52 .... $1,000.00 – 1,200.00
Plate 455
Portrait plaque, 9½" T., green mark #47 .... $600.00 – 700.00
Plate 456
Portrait wine jugs, each 9½" T., blue mark #52 ......(Each) $1,050.00 – 1,200.00

PAGES 74 and 75

Plate 457
Portrait vase, 12½" T., blue mark #52.............................. $1,000.00 – 1,200.00
Plate 458
Portrait candlestick, 9" T., blue mark #52 .... $400.00 – 500.00
Plate 459
Portrait vase, 12" T., blue mark #52 .... $1,100.00 – 1,300.00
Plate 460
Portrait covered urn, 10½" T., blue mark #52 .... $1,200.00 – 1,400.00
Plate 461
Portrait vase, 18¼" T., blue mark #52.............................. $2,000.00 – 2,500.00
Plate 462
Portrait cream & sugar, sugar 3½" T. w/finial, green mark #52 $400.00 – 500.00
Plate 463
Portrait vase, 7" T., blue mark #52 .... $650.00 – 800.00
Plate 464
Portrait ewer, 6½" T., green mark #52 .... $600.00 – 700.00
Plate 465
Portrait vase, 9" T., blue mark #52 .... $750.00 – 900.00
Portrait vase, 8¾" T., blue mark #52 .... $700.00 – 850.00

PAGES 76 and 77

Plate 466
Moriage vase, 9¼" T., mark #70 .... $425.00 – 500.00
Plate 467
Moriage vase, 7½" T., blue mark #47 .... $400.00 – 475.00
Plate 468
Moriage tankard, 12" T., blue mark #52 .... $475.00 – 575.00
Plate 469
Moriage vase, 5" W., 2" T., blue mark #52 .... $200.00 – 260.00
Plate 470
Moriage vase, 7" T., green mark #52 .... $300.00 – 375.00
Moriage vase, 9½" T., blue mark #52 .... $400.00 – 500.00
Plate 471
Moriage vase, 9" T., 9" W., blue mark #52 .... $500.00 – 600.00
Plate 472
Moriage creamer and sugar, sugar 4¼" T. including finial,
green mark #90... $235.00 – 300.00

Moriage vase, 7" T., green mark #9 .... $325.00 – 400.00
Plate 473
Moriage vase, 8½" W., 3" T., blue mark #52 .... $325.00 – 400.00
Plate 474
Moriage vase, 7" T., blue mark #52 .... $400.00 – 475.00
Plate 475
Moriage vase, 8½" T., green mark #52 .... $350.00 – 450.00

PAGES 78 and 79

Plate 476
Moriage vase, 9¼" T., blue mark #52 .... $350.00 – 425.00
Plate 477
Moriage vase, 7" T., green mark #52 .... $275.00 – 350.00
Plate 478
Moriage urn, 11" T., 2 pc., blue mark #90 .... $450.00 – 550.00
Moriage tankard, 10" T., blue mark #52 .... $400.00 – 425.00
Plate 479
Moriage vase, molded in relief, 6" T., green mark #47 ...... $500.00 – 600.00
Plate 480
Moriage ferner, molded in relief, 6" W., green mark #47 .. $500.00 – 600.00
Plate 481
Moriage tankard, 14¼" T., blue mark #52 .... $600.00 – 700.00
Plate 482
Moriage covered urn, 11" T., green mark #52 .... $525.00 – 625.00
Plate 483
Moriage vase, 8½" T., green mark #52 .... $300.00 – 375.00
Plate 484
Moriage vase, molded in relief, 9½" T., green mark #47.... $500.00 – 600.00

PAGES 80 and 81

Plate 485
Moriage vase, 5¼" T., blue mark #70 .... $225.00 – 275.00
Plate 486
Moriage vase, 6½" T., blue mark #52 .... $225.00 – 275.00
Plate 487
Moriage teapot, 6½" T., green mark #71 .... $225.00 – 275.00
Plate 488
Moriage creamer, 5" T., blue mark #52 .... $100.00 – 140.00
Plate 489
Moriage vase, 10½" T., blue mark #52 .... $375.00 – 450.00
Plate 490
Moriage vase, 13½" T., blue mark #52 .... $475.00 – 550.00
Plate 491
Moriage vase, 10" T., green mark #52 .... $325.00 – 400.00
Plate 492
Moriage vase, note jewels on wings, 9" T., blue mark #52 .. $350.00 – 425.00
Plate 493
Moriage vase, 9" T., blue mark #90 .... $325.00 – 400.00
Plate 494
Moriage vase, 12½" T., blue mark #52 .... $400.00 – 500.00
Plate 495
Moriage vase, 6" T., blue mark #52 .... $275.00 – 350.00
Moriage vase, 7" T., green mark #52 .... $300.00 – 375.00
Plate 496
Moriage ewer, 7½" T., blue mark #47 .... $300.00 – 375.00
Moriage hanging plaque, 7¾" dia., blue mark #47 .... $200.00 – 250.00

PAGES 82 and 83

Plate 497
Moriage chocolate set, pot 9" T., set comes w/five cups
and saucers, green mark #47 .... $650.00 – 750.00
Plate 498
Moriage pitcher 6" T., blue mark #52 .... $200.00 – 270.00
Plate 499
Moriage tankard, 15¾" T., mark #70 .... $800.00 – 900.00
Plate 500
Moriage ewer, 9" T., mark #24 .... $275.00 – 350.00
Plate 501
Moriage pitcher, 7" T., blue mark #52 .... $225.00 – 300.00
Plate 502
Moriage mug, 5½" T., blue mark #52 .... $200.00 – 270.00
Plate 503
Moriage ewer, 7½" T., blue mark #90 .... $350.00 – 400.00
Plate 504
Moriage vase, 8¼" T., blue mark #52 .... $450.00 – 525.00

Plate 505
Moriage humidor, 8" T., blue mark #52 .... $525.00 – 625.00
Moriage wine jug, 8" T., blue mark #52 .... $750.00 – 850.00

PAGES 84 and 85

Plate 506
Moriage vase, 8½" T., blue mark #52 .... $375.00 – 450.00
Plate 507
Moriage sugar and creamer, sugar bowl 4½" T. incl. finial,
mark #16 .... $200.00 – 250.00
Plate 508
Moriage hanging plaque, 9½", green mark #52 .... $350.00 – 425.00
Plate 509
Moriage lemonade set, set has pitcher 6½" T., five cups
3¾" T., green mark #101 .... $400.00 – 500.00
Plate 510
Moriage vase, 5½" T., green mark #52 .... $225.00 – 275.00
Plate 511
Moriage cracker or cookie jar, 8" T., blue mark #52 .... $350.00 – 425.00
Plate 512
Moriage tea set, pot 5½" T., incl. finial, set has creamer,
sugar, six cups and saucers, green mark #47 .... $625.00 – 750.00
Plate 513
Moriage covered urn, 14½" T., blue mark #52 .... $850.00 – 950.00
Plate 514
Moriage tea set, pot 6¾" T. w/finial, set has teapot, sugar,
creamer, six cups and saucers, mark #73 .... $750.00 – 850.00

PAGES 86 and 87

Plate 515
Moriage vase, 9" T., blue mark #90 .... $300.00 – 400.00
Plate 516
Moriage vase, 8¾" T., blue mark #90 .... $300.00 – 400.00
Plate 517
Moriage vase, 3½" T. x 5½" dia., blue mark #90 .... $175.00 – 225.00
Plate 518
Moriage compote, 5" W. incl. handles, blue mark #90 ...... $75.00 – 125.00
Moriage vase, 4¾" T., blue mark #90 .... $175.00 – 225.00
Plate 519
Moriage vases, 6" T., green mark #47 ....(Each) $125.00 – 175.00
Plate 520
Moriage creamer and sugar, sugar bowl 3½" T. w/finial,
green mark #47 .... $165.00 – 225.00
Plate 521
Moriage vase, 6" T., green mark #52 .... $150.00 – 200.00
Plate 522
Moriage vase, 7" T., green mark #90 .... $325.00 – 375.00
Moriage humidor, 6½" T., blue mark #90 .... $450.00 – 525.00
Plate 523
Moriage humidor, also molded in relief, 6½" T., green
mark #47 .... $550.00 – 625.00
Plate 524
Moriage ashtray, 5½" W., green mark #47 .... $125.00 – 160.00
Moriage mug, 5½" T., green mark #47 .... $200.00 – 275.00
Plate 525
Moriage ashtray, 5¼" W., green mark #47 .... $150.00 – 200.00
Plate 526
Moriage vase, 12½" T., green mark #47 .... $275.00 – 350.00
Moriage vase, 8½" T., blue mark #52 .... $250.00 – 325.00
Plate 527
Moriage tea set, pot 6¾" T., creamer 3¾" T., sugar 5"
T. incl. finial, green mark #71 .... $325.00 – 425.00

PAGES 88 and 89

Plate 528
Hanging plaque, molded in relief, 12" W.,green mark #47.. $1,600.00 – 1,900.00
Plate 529
Humidor, molded in relief, 6½" T., green mark #47........... $700.00 – 800.00
Plate 530
Sugar and creamer, molded in relief, sugar bowl 4½" T.
incl. finial, green mark #47 .... $225.00 – 275.00
Plate 531
Humidor, molded in relief, 7½" T., mark #47 .... $1,600.00 – 1,800.00
Plate 532
Humidor, molded in relief, 7" T., green mark #47 .... $1,100.00 – 1,300.00

Plate 533
Humidor, molded in relief, 6¾" T., green mark #47 .... $900.00 – 1,000.00
Plate 534
Humidor, molded in relief, 7¼" T., green mark #47............ $850.00 – 950.00
Plate 535
Humidor, molded in relief, 7¼" T., green mark #47............ $2,400.00 – 2,700.00

PAGES 90 and 91

Plate 536
Top Row:
Nut bowl, molded in relief, 7¾" W., green mark #47.......... $125.00 – 175.00
Bottom Row:
Nut bowl, molded in relief, 8¾" W., green mark #47.......... $125.00 – 175.00
Plate 537
Humidor, molded in relief, 6¼" T., (see plates #539 & 545
for different decoration of same mold) green mark #47 .... $750.00 – 950.00
Plate 538
Nut bowls, molded in relief, both 8½" W., w/green mark
#47 ....(Each) $140.00 – 200.00
Plate 539
Humidor, molded in relief, 6¼" T., (see plates #537 & 545
for different decoration of same mold), green mark #47.... $750.00 – 950.00
Plate 540
Humidor, molded in relief, 6¼" T., blue mark #110 .... $1,100.00 – 1,300.00
Plate 541
Humidor, molded in relief, 7¼" T., green mark #47............ $850.00 – 1,000.00
Plate 542
Humidor, molded in relief, 7¼" T., green mark #47............ $1,000.00 – 1,200.00
Plate 543
Humidor, molded in relief, 6½" T., green mark #47 .... $850.00 – 1,000.00
Plate 544
Humidor, molded in relief, 6½" T., green mark #47 (not
original cover) .... $900.00 – 1,100.00
Plate 545
Humidor, molded in relief, 6¼" T., (see plates #537 & 539
for different decoration of same mold), green mark #47.... $750.00 – 950.00

PAGES 92 and 93

Plate 546
Top Row:
Nut bowl, molded in relief, 4½" W., green mark #47 .... $100.00 – 140.00
Bottom Row:
Nut bowl, molded in relief, 7½" W., green mark #47 .... $125.00 – 175.00
Plate 547
Top Row:
Nut bowl, molded in relief, 7½" W., green mark #47 .... $125.00 – 175.00
Bottom Row:
Nut bowl, molded in relief, 7½" W., green mark #47 .... $125.00 – 175.00
Plate 548
Humidor, molded in relief, 7½" T., green mark #47............ $900.00 – 1,000.00
Plate 549
Vase, molded in relief, 8" T., (see front view in plate #553),
green mark #47.. $800.00 – 1,000.00
Plate 550
Humidor, molded in relief, 7½" T., blue mark #52 .... $700.00 – 850.00
Plate 551
Ashtray, molded in relief, 5¼" W., (see plate #555 for dif-
ferent decoration of same mold), green mark #47 .... $300.00 – 400.00
Plate 552
Humidor, molded in relief, 7½" T., green mark #47............ $1,100.00 – 1,300.00
Plate 553
Vase, molded in relief, 8" T., (see rear view in plate #549),
green mark #47.. $900.00 – 1,100.00
Plate 554
Hanging plaque, molded in relief,10"dia., green mark #47 .. $1,200.00 – 1,400.00
Plate 555
Ashtrays, molded in relief, 5¼" W., (see plate #551 for dif-
ferent decoration of same mold), green mark #47 ..(Each) $300.00 – 400.00
Plate 556
Hanging plaque, molded in relief,10"dia., green mark #47 .. $1,000.00 – 1,100.00
Plate 557
Hanging plaque, molded in relief, 10½" dia., green mark #47.. $900.00 – 1,100.00

PAGES 94 and 95

Plate 558
Rose bowl, molded in relief, 3½" T., green mark #47 .... $250.00 – 325.00

Plate 559
Vase, molded in relief, 9¾" T., green mark #47 .... $2,000.00 – 2,400.00
Plate 560
Vase, molded in relief, 12½" T., blue mark #52 .... $4,500.00 – 5,200.00
Plate 561
Nut bowl, molded in relief, 5¾" W., green mark #47 .... $100.00 – 140.00
Plate 562
Nut bowl, molded in relief, 7" W., green mark #47 .... $175.00 – 250.00
Plate 563
Nut bowl, molded in relief, 7½" W., handles, green
mark #47.. $125.00 – 175.00
Plate 564
Vase, molded in relief, 8½" T., blue mark #52 .... $500.00 – 600.00
Plate 565
Vase, molded in relief, 10½" T., green mark #47 .... $450.00 – 550.00
Plate 566
Wine jug, molded in relief, 11" T., green mark #47 .... $5,200.00 – 6,000.00
Plate 567
Vase, molded in relief, 7" T., blue mark #52 .... $500.00 – 700.00
Plate 568
Charger, molded in relief, 13½" W., green mark #47 .... $2,000.00 – 2,400.00
Plate 569
Basket, molded in relief, 7½" W., green mark #47 .... $350.00 – 425.00
Vase, molded in relief, 7½" T., green mark #47 .... $400.00 – 500.00
Plate 570
Ashtray-matchbox holder combination, molded in relief,
5¼" L. and 4½" T., green mark #47................................... $450.00 – 550.00

PAGES 96 and 97

Plate 571
Decanter, heavily beaded, 7" T., mark #10....................... $300.00 – 400.00
Plate 572
Cookie or cracker jar, heavily beaded, 7" T., 8" W., blue
mark #52.. $450.00 – 600.00
Plate 573
Vase, heavily beaded, 7½" T., green mark #52 .... $425.00 – 500.00
Plate 574
Vase, "sponge" tapestry, 8¼" T., blue mark #52................ $425.00 – 525.00
Plate 575
Vase, "sponge" tapestry, 8½" T., blue mark #52................ $425.00 – 525.00
Plate 576
Vase, heavily beaded, 7½" T., unmarked .... $400.00 – 500.00
Plate 577
Vase, heavily beaded, 6" T., blue mark #52 .... $325.00 – 425.00
Plate 578
Berry set, heavily beaded, large bowl is 10½" dia., small
bowls are 5" dia., blue mark #52....................................... $425.00 – 525.00
Plate 579
Candlestick, heavily beaded, 10¾" T., blue mark #52 ...... $235.00 – 280.00

PAGES 98 and 99

Plate 580
Bowl, imitation Gouda-style, 8" W., green mark #47 .... $125.00 – 165.00
Plate 581
Compote, supported by three griffins, triangular shaped
base, 8" W. x 5" T., green mark #47 .... $450.00 – 550.00
Plate 582
Egg warmer, souvenir, marked "Watergap, Pa." 5½" W.,
green mark #47.. $140.00 – 180.0
Plate 583
Sardine set, three-piece, w/figural sardine sprigged
on top, 6¼" L., green mark #47... $160.00 – 225.00
Plate 584
Figural bird, 4¼" T., green mark #47................................. $225.00 – 300.00
Plate 585
Vase, coralene, 9½" T., mark #95..................................... $350.00 – 425.00
Plate 586
Souvenir "Nipper" figural, marked "Souvenir of Colorado
Springs, Colo.", 4½" L., green mark #26 .... $175.00 – 225.00
Plate 587
Bridge ashtray set, four-piece, each approx. 4" W., blue
mark #84.. $500.00 – 625.00
Plate 588
Figural bunny light, 6¼" T., green mark #47 .... $1,500.00 – 1,800.00
Figural owl light, 6¼" T., green mark #47 .... $1,500.00 – 1,800.00
Plate 589
Figural matchbox holder, 3" T., incised w/mark #55 .... $250.00 – 350.00

Plate 590
  Figural tea set, set has pot 4" T. incl. finial, creamer,
  sugar, six cups and saucers, green mark #47 .... $750.00 – 900.00

PAGES 100 and 101

Plate 591
Top Row:
  Figural monkey, 4½" T., mark #55 .... $200.00 – 250.00
Bottom Row:
  Figural bird, 5" L., green mark #47 .... $225.00 – 300.00
  Figural bird toothpick holder, 3" T., green mark #47 .... $225.00 – 300.00
  Figural bird, 4½" L., green mark #47 .... $225.00 – 300.00
Plate 592
  Figural of three monkeys, "see no evil, hear no evil, speak
  no evil" 4" W., 2½" high, incised w/mark #55 .... $175.00 – 225.00
Plate 593
  Figural owl and tree vase, 9" T., green mark #47 .... $1,000.00 – 1,300.00
Plate 594
  Figural seal ashtray, tray 7" L., seal 3½" T., green
  mark #47 .... $525.00 – 625.00
Plate 595
  Figural ashtray, 6" W., green mark #47 .... $500.00 – 600.00
Plate 596
  Figural penguin ashtray, 6" W. x 5" T., green mark #47 .... $625.00 – 700.00
Plate 597
  Figural fox ashtray, 6½" L., green mark #47 .... $425.00 – 500.00
Plate 598
  Figural dog ashtray and combination matchbox holder, 5"
  W., 4" deep, green mark #47 .... $425.00 – 500.00
Plate 599
  Figural pipe ashtray, 4½" W., green mark #47 .... $225.00 – 300.00
Plate 600
  Figural kingfisher ashtray, 6½" W., green mark #47 .... $700.00 – 800.00

PAGES 102 and 103

Plate 601
  Figural bird on small dish, 6" W., blue mark #84 .... $75.00 – 135.00
  Figural egg trinket box w/heavy moriage trim, 6" L., green
  mark #47 .... $300.00 – 375.00
  Figural lion on side of ashtray, 4½" W., green mark
  #47 .... $300.00 – 400.00
Plate 602
  Figural boy ashtray, 3½" W., 2½" T., blue mark #84 .... $150.00 – 200.00
Plate 603
  Figural incense burner, 6" T., mark #55 .... $250.00 – 300.00
  Figural incense burner, 8" T., mark #55 .... $250.00 – 300.00
  Figural incense burner, 5" T., mark #55 .... $200.00 – 250.00
Plate 604
  Figural bird on relish dish, 7¾" W., green mark #47 .... $150.00 – 225.00
Plate 605
  Doll, 24" T., mark #133 .... $425.00 – 500.00
Plate 606
  Doll 20" T., mark #123 .... $350.00 – 400.00
Plate 607
  Doll, 15" T., mark #121 .... $250.00 – 325.00
Plate 608
  Doll, 24" T., mark #128 .... $425.00 – 500.00
Plate 609
  Doll, 15½" T., mark #133 .... $250.00 – 325.00

PAGES 104 and 105

Plate 610
  Doll, 24" T., mark #153 .... $425.00 – 500.00
Plate 611
  Doll, 13" T., mark #155 .... $225.00 – 275.00
Plate 612
  Doll, 12" T., mark #121 .... $225.00 – 275.00
Plate 613
  Doll, 12" T., mark #122 .... $225.00 – 275.00
Plate 614
  Doll, 9" T., mark #55 .... $165.00 – 225.00
Plate 615
  Doll, 4½" T., mark #55.. $100.00 – 140.00
Plate 616
  Twin dolls, 3½" T., mark #55 ....(Each) $90.00 – 130.00

Plate 617
  Doll, 5" T., mark #144 .... $110.00 – 150.00
  Doll, 5¼" T., mark #147.. $110.00 – 150.00
Plate 618
  Doll, 9" T., mark #55 .... $175.00 – 225.00

PAGES 106 and 107

Plate 619
  Doll, 4¾" T., mark #55 .... $125.00 – 175.00
  Doll, 4¾" T., mark #55 .... $125.00 – 175.00
Plate 620
  Doll, 6" T., mark #55 .... $125.00 – 175.00
Plate 621
  Doll, 5" T., mark #55 .... $125.00 – 160.00
Plate 622
  Doll, 4¼" T., mark #55 .... $125.00 – 160.00
  Doll, 3¾" T., mark #55 .... $100.00 – 135.00
Plate 623
  Doll, 5½" T., mark #55 .... $125.00 – 160.00
  Doll, 4" T., mark #55 .... $100.00 – 140.00
Plate 624
  Doll, 4" T., mark #55 .... $100.00 – 140.00
Plate 625
  Doll, 6" T., mark #55 .... $125.00 – 160.00
  Doll, 6½" T., mark #55 .... $125.00 – 160.00
Plate 626
  Doll, 5" T., mark #55 .... $125.00 – 160.00
  Doll, 5¼" T., mark #55 .... $125.00 – 160.00
Plate 627
  Doll, 5¼" T., mark #55 .... $125.00 – 160.00
  Doll, 4¼" T., mark #55 .... $100.00 – 140.00
Plate 628
  Doll, 5" T., mark #55 .... $125.00 – 160.00

PAGES 108 and 109

Plate 629
  Doll, 4½" T., mark #55.. $125.00 – 175.00
Plate 630
  Doll, 4¾" T., mark #55 .... $125.00 – 175.00
  Doll, 4¾" T., mark #55 .... $125.00 – 175.00
Plate 631
  "Dolly" doll w/original sticker (#13), 3½" T., mark #55........ $125.00 – 160.00
  Doll, 3¼" T., mark #55 .... $110.00 – 140.00
Plate 632
  Doll, 3¾" T., mark #55 .... $100.00 – 130.00
Plate 633
  Doll, 6¾" T., mark #55 .... $125.00 – 175.00
  Doll, 7" T., mark #55 .... $125.00 – 175.00
Plate 634
  Doll, 6¼" T., mark #55 .... $125.00 – 175.00
  Doll, 5¾" T., mark #55 .... $125.00 – 175.00
Plate 635
  Doll, 4¼" T., mark #55 .... $110.00 – 140.00
  Doll, 7" T., cloth body, mark #55..................................... $125.00 – 175.00
Plate 636
  Doll, 6½" T., mark #55 .... $125.00 – 175.00
  Doll, 6½" T., mark #55 .... $125.00 – 175.00
Plate 637
  Doll, 5¼" T., mark #55 .... $110.00 – 140.00
Plate 638
  Doll, 5" T., mark #55 .... $110.00 – 140.00
  Doll, 4" T., mark #55 .... $90.00 – 130.00

PAGES 110 and 111

Plate 639
  Doll, 4¼" T., mark #55.. $110.00 – 140.00
  Doll, 3¼" T., mark #55.. $100.00 – 130.00
Plate 640
  Doll, 4¼" T., mark #55.. $150.00 – 185.00
  Doll, 5¼" T., mark #55.. $150.00 – 185.00
Plate 641
  Doll, 4½" T., mark #55.. $110.00 – 140.00
  Doll, 4½" T., mark #55.. $110.00 – 140.00
Plate 642
  Doll, 5" T., mark #55 .... $110.00 – 140.00

244

Doll, 7¼" T., mark #55 .... $125.00 – 160.00
Plate 643
    Doll, 5½" T., mark #55 .... $125.00 – 160.00
Plate 644
    Doll, 4½" T., mark #55 .... $125.00 – 160.00
Plate 645
    Doll, 4½" T., mark #55 .... $135.00 – 175.00
    Doll, 4½" T., mark #55 .... $150.00 – 185.00
Plate 646
    Doll, 4½" T., mark #55 .... $150.00 – 185.00

PAGES 112 and 113

Plate 647
    Doll, 4" T., mark #55 .... $125.00 – 160.00
Plate 648
    Dolls, smallest is 3¾" T., large is 5¾" T., mark #55 (Small) $90.00 – 125.00
    ....(Large) $125.00 – 160.00
Plate 649
    Doll, 6" T., mark #55 .... $110.00 – 150.00
Plate 650
    Doll, 3½" T., mark #55 .... $135.00 – 165.00
Plate 651
    Doll, 5½" T., mark #55 .... $100.00 – 140.00
    Doll, 6½" T., mark #55 .... $110.00 – 160.00
Plate 652
    Doll, 4½" T., mark #55 .... $110.00 – 140.00
    Doll, 4¾" T., mark #55 .... $110.00 – 140.00
Plate 653
    Doll, 3½" T., mark #55 .... $100.00 – 140.00
Plate 654
    Doll, 4¼" T., mark #55 .... $100.00 – 140.00
    Doll, 4½" T., mark #55 .... $100.00 – 140.00
Plate 655
    Twin dolls, 4½" T., mark #55 ....(Each) $110.00 – 140.00
Plate 656
    Large Baby Bud doll, 7" T., mark #55 .... $160.00 – 200.00
Plate 657
    Doll, 4½" T., mark #55 .... $125.00 – 160.00

PAGES 114 and 115

Plate 658
    Baby doll w/bottle, jointed arm allows bottle to go in mouth, 3½" T., mark #55 .... $110.00 – 150.00
Plate 659
    Doll, 5" T., mark #55 .... $110.00 – 140.00
    Doll, 4½" T., mark #55 .... $120.00 – 160.00
Plate 660
    Doll, 4¾" T., mark #55 .... $120.00 – 160.00
Plate 661
    Doll, 5¼" T., mark #55 .... $120.00 – 160.00
Plate 662
    Doll, 3¾" T., mark #55 .... $110.00 – 140.00
    Doll, 3¾" T., mark #55 .... $110.00 – 140.00
Plate 663
    Doll, 5" T., mark #55 .... $110.00 – 140.00
    Kewpie doll, 5" T., mark #55 .... $130.00 – 170.00
Plate 664
    Doll, 4¾" T., mark #55 .... $100.00 – 140.00
    Doll, 5" T., mark #55 .... $100.00 – 140.00
Plate 665
    Ballerina doll, 3¼" T., mark #55 .... $120.00 – 160.00
Plate 666
    Twin dolls, 4¼" T., mark #55 ....(Each) $100.00 – 140.00
Plate 667
    Twin dolls, one dressed, one undressed, 5" T., mark #144 ....(Each) $110.00 – 150.00
Plate 668
    Baby doll w/bottle, jointed arm allows bottle to go in mouth, 5½" T., mark #55 .... $110.00 – 150.00

PAGES 116 and 117

Plate 669
    Kewpie doll, 5¾" T., mark #55 .... $150.00 – 200.00
Plate 670
    Doll, 4¾" T., mark #55 .... $110.00 – 150.00

Doll, 5" mark #145 .... $110.00 – 150.00
Plate 671
    Doll, 4¾" T., mark #55 .... $110.00 – 150.00
    Doll, 4½" T., mark #55 .... $110.00 – 150.00
Plate 672
    Doll, 5¼" T., mark #146 .... $110.00 – 150.00
    Doll, 5½" T., mark #55 .... $110.00 – 150.00
Plate 673
    "Queue San Baby," 5" T., w/sticker #78 on front, mark #55 .... $175.00 – 225.00
    "Sonny" doll, 5" T., w/sticker #158 on front, mark #55 ...... $175.00 – 225.00
Plate 674
    Doll, 4" T., mark #55 .... $100.00 – 140.00
    Doll, 4¼" T., mark #55 .... $100.00 – 140.00
Plate 675
    Doll, 4½" T., mark #55 .... $100.00 – 140.00
    Doll, 5" T., mark #55 .... $100.00 – 140.00
Plate 676
    Doll in bathtub, doll 1¾" L. x 2½" T., tub 3" L. x 1½" T., both incised w/mark #55 .... $100.00 – 140.00
Plate 677
    Kewpie doll 4¼" T., w/red and gold sticker "Kewpie, Reg. U.S. Off.," mark #55 .... $150.00 – 200.00
    Kewpie doll, 5¼" T., w/red and gold sticker "Kewpie, Reg. U.S. Off.," mark #55 .... $160.00 – 210.00
Plate 678
    Doll in bathtub, doll 1½" T., tub 2½" L., tub incised w/mark #55 .... $100.00 – 140.00
Plate 679
    Same as #678 .... $100.00 – 140.00

PAGES 118 and 119

Plate 680
    Doll, 6" T., mark #55 .... $125.00 – 160.00
    Doll, 5¾" T., mark #55 .... $125.00 – 160.00
Plate 681
    Doll, 6" T., mark #58 .... $110.00 – 150.00
    Doll, 5½" T., mark #141 .... $110.00 – 140.00
Plate 682
    Half doll w/sew holes, 2½" T., mark #55 .... $125.00 – 175.00
    Half doll w/sew holes, 2½" T., mark #55 .... $125.00 – 175.00
Plate 683
    Child's dresser set, hatpin holder 2" T., blue mark #84 .... $250.00 – 325.00
Plate 684
    Ladykin doll, 3½" T., w/sticker #138, mark #55 .... $150.00 – 200.00
Plate 685
    Rear view of plate #684 showing sticker .... $150.00 – 200.00
Plate 686
    Rear view of Jollikid doll, 3¾" T., w/sticker #137, mark #55 $150.00 – 200.00
Plate 687
    Doll head, 1¾" T., mark #55 .... $70.00 – 90.00
Plate 688
    Doll head, 1¾" T., mark #55 .... $70.00 – 90.00
Plate 689
    Front view of Jollikid doll, plate #686 .... $150.00 – 200.00
Plate 690
    Child's play tea set, set has teapot, creamer, sugar, four cups, saucers and plates; pot 4" T., blue mark #84 .... $225.00 – 300.00

PAGES 120 and 121

Plate 691
    Child's feeding dish, 7" W., blue mark #84 .... $75.00 – 100.00
Plate 692
    Child's play tea set, has teapot, creamer, sugar, four cups and saucers; pot 3½" T., blue mark #84 .... $250.00 – 325.00
Plate 693
    Child's play tea set, has teapot, creamer, sugar, six cups, saucers and plates; pot 3¼" T., cups 1½" T., blue mark #84 .. $225.00 – 300.00
Plate 694
    Child's feeding dishes, all have blue mark #84
        Plate, 6½" W. .... $35.00 – 55.00
        Cup, 2½" T., ... $75.00 – 100.00
        Creamer, 3¼" T., ... $50.00 – 75.00
Plate 695
    Child's play tea set, with Sunbonnet Babies, has teapot, creamer, sugar, six cups, saucers and plates, blue mark #66 .... $300.00 – 400.00

Plate 696
    Child's egg cup, 2½" T., blue mark #84 .... $60.00 – 80.00
Plate 697
    Child's play tea set, has teapot, creamer, sugar, four cups,
    saucers, and plates, blue mark #84 .... $250.00 – 325.00
Plate 698
    Child's dresser set, each 2¾" W., green mark #47............ $135.00 – 175.00
Plate 699
    Child's play tea set, has teapot, creamer, sugar, six cups,
    saucers and plates, blue mark #84 .... $250.00 – 325.00
Plate 700
    Child's play tea set, has teapot, creamer, sugar, four cups,
    saucers and plates, blue mark #84 .... $250.00 – 325.00
Plate 701
    Child's candlestick, 5½" T., green mark #47 .... $110.00 – 160.00

PAGES 122 and 123

Plate 702
    Child's feeding dish, 7" W., green mark #8......................... $75.00 – 100.00
Plate 703
    Child's feeding set:
    Feeding dish, 6¾" W. .... $75.00 – 100.00
    Plate, 6½" W. .... $35.00 – 50.00
    Bowl, 4¾" W. .... $50.00 – 75.00
    Creamer, 3" T., blue mark #84 .... $50.00 – 75.00
Plate 704
    Child's play creamer and sugar set, sugar bowl 2½" T.
    including finial, blue mark #84... $65.00 – 100.00
Plate 705
    Child's play creamer and sugar set, sugar bowl 3" T.
    including finial, mark #10 .... $35.00 – 50.00
Plate 706
    Child's chamberstick, 1½" T., green mark #47 .... $85.00 – 120.00
Plate 707
    Child's play tea set, has teapot, creamer, sugar, four cups,
    saucers and plates; teapot 4" T., blue mark #84 .... $225.00 – 300.00
Plate 708
    Child's play tea set, has teapot 3½" T., creamer, sugar,
    four cups, saucers and plates, blue mark #84 .... $250.00 – 325.00
Plate 709
    Child's dresser set, tray 6" L. x 4" W., hatpin holder 1¾"
    T., hair receiver 2½" W., mark #113 .... $150.00 – 225.00
Plate 710
    Child's play tea set, has teapot 3½" T., creamer, sugar,
    six cups, saucers and plates, blue mark #84 .... $250.00 – 325.00
Plate 711
    Child's feeding dish, 8" W., blue mark #84 .... $75.00 – 100.00

PAGES 124 and 125

Plate 712
    Small dish from tea set, 4¾" W., green mark #8................ $10.00 – 15.00
Plate 713
    Child's mug, 2½" T., blue mark #84 .... $65.00 – 95.00
Plate 714
    Doll face pattern items;
    On left, tiny tea set, cups 1" dia. x 1" T., saucers 1⅝"
    W., creamer 1¼" T., sugar 1⅝" T., teapot 2⅞" T.;
    blue mark #55 stamped on bottom of pieces .... $225.00 – 300.00
    On right, bigger tea set, cups 1¼" T. x 1¼" dia., saucers
    2½" dia., covered sugar 2½" T., teapot 3¼" T., blue
    mark #55 stamped on bottom of pieces .... $150.00 – 200.00
Plate 715
    Doll face pattern items, child's breakfast set all with blue
    #84
    Fruit bowl, 5¼" W. .... $75.00 – 100.00
    Egg cup, 3½" T... $75.00 – 100.00
    Cereal bowl, 5¾" W. .... $75.00 – 100.00
    Mug, 2¾" T. .... $75.00 – 100.00
    Plate, 5¾" W. .... $75.00 – 100.00
    Creamer, 3" T. .... $75.00 – 100.00
Plate 716
    Doll face pattern items, both w/blue mark #84
    On left, powder box, 4" W. x 3" T....................................... $85.00 – 125.00
    On right, heart-shaped dish, 5¼" W. .... $85.00 – 125.00
Plate 717
    Doll face pattern hanging plaque, 6⅛" W., blue
    mark #84 .... $75.00 – 100.00

Plate 718
    Doll face pattern mugs:
    Large 3" dia., medium 2¾" dia., small 2½" dia., all have
    blue mark #84..(Each) $50.00 – 75.00
Plate 719
    Doll face pattern cup and saucer, cup 2⅛" T., saucer
    5" blue mark #84.. $50.00 – 75.00

PAGES 126 and 127

All With American Indian Decoration.

Plate 720
    Ashtray, 5¼" dia., green mark #47 .... $200.00 – 250.00
    Humidor, 4" T., green mark #47 .... $450.00 – 525.00
    Nappy, 5½" dia., green mark #47 .... $150.00 – 200.00
Plate 721
    Creamer, 2½" T., green mark #47 .... $120.00 – 150.00
    Ashtray, 4¾" W., green mark #47 .... $150.00 – 200.00
Plate 722
    Vase, 14" T., green mark #47 .... $800.00 – 1,000.00
Plate 723
    Hanging plaque, 10½" W., blue mark #52 .... $1,000.00 – 1,300.00
Plate 724
    Humidor, molded in relief, 6½" T., green mark #47 ....$1,100.00 – 1,300.00
Plate 725
    Humidor, 5½" T., blue mark #47 .... $1,000.00 – 1,200.00
Plate 726
    Ashtray, molded in relief, 6½" L., green mark #47 .... $800.00 – 1,000.00
Plate 727
    Ashtray, 5½" W., green mark #47 .... $450.00 – 550.00
Plate 728
    Ferner, molded in relief, 6¾" T., 6" W., green mark #47.... $800.00 – 1,000.00
Plate 729
    Humidor, molded in relief, 7¾" T., green mark #47............$1,300.00 – 1,500.00

PAGES 128 and 129

Plate 730
    Wine jug, Indian in canoe, 8¾" T., green mark #47 .... $850.00 – 950.00
Plate 731
    Cracker jar, Indian in canoe, 8½" dia., green mark #47 .... $300.00 – 400.00
Plate 732
    Vase, Indian in canoe, 7" T., green mark #47.................... $300.00 – 375.00
Plate 733
    Tea set, Indian in canoe, has teapot, creamer, sugar, six
    cups and saucers; pot 4½" T., green mark #109 .... $600.00 – 700.00
Plate 734
    Nut dish, Indian in canoe, 5½" W., green mark #47 .... $150.00 – 200.00
Plate 735
    Hanging plaque, 11" W., green mark #47......................... $500.00 – 600.00
Plate 736
    Humidor, 6" T., green mark #47 .... $550.00 – 625.00
Plate 737
    Vase, Indian in canoe, 12½" T., blue mark #52 .... $450.00 – 525.00
Plate 738
    Ferner, Indian in canoe, 8" L., green mark #47 .... $300.00 – 375.00
Plate 739
    Celery dish, Indian in canoe, 12" L., green mark #47 .... $175.00 – 225.00
Plate 740
    Hanging plaque, 10" W., green mark #47......................... $500.00 – 600.00

PAGES 130 and 131

Plate 741
    Serving dish, two-tier, 8½" W., Indian in canoe, mark #17.. $200.00 – 275.00
Plate 742
    Bowl, Indian in canoe, 7½" W., green mark #47 .... $150.00 – 200.00
Plate 743
    Hanging plaque, man on camel scene, 10" W., green
    mark #47.. $300.00 – 400.00
Plate 744
    Inkwell set, three-piece, has insert; man on camel scene,
    2¾" W., green mark #47 .... $200.00 – 250.00
Plate 745
    Stein, man on camel scene, 7" T., green mark #47 .... $600.00 – 700.00
Plate 746
    Vase, man on camel scene, 9" T., green mark #47 .... $400.00 – 475.00

Vase, man on camel scene, 7" T., green marl #47 .... $325.00 – 400.00
Plate 747
    Vases, man on camel scene, 6" T., green mark
    #47 ....(Each) $250.00 – 325.00
Plate 748
    Vase, man on camel scene, 18" T., green mark #47 .... $2,000.00 – 2,500.00
Plate 749
    Hanging plaque, man on camel scene, 10" W., green
    mark #47 .... $300.00 – 400.00
    Hanging plaque, man on camel scene, 10" W., green
    mark #47 .... $300.00 – 400.00
Plate 750
    Mug, man on camel scene, some moriage trim, 4¾" T.,
    green mark #47 .... $250.00 – 325.00

PAGES 132 and 133

Plate 751
    Vase, man on camel scene, 18" T., green mark #47 .... $1,300.00 – 1,800.00
Plate 752
    Cigarette box, man on camel scene, 4½" L., green mark
    #47 .... $250.00 – 325.00
Plate 753
    Vase, man on camel scene, some moriage trim, 12½" T.,
    green mark #47 .... $650.00 – 800.00
Plate 754
    Chocolate set, man on camel scene, has chocolate pot
    9½" T., four cups and saucers, green mark #47 .... $900.00 – 1,100.00
Plate 755
    Fruit bowl, man on camel scene, 12" W., green mark #47 $350.00 – 425.00
Plate 756
    Vase, man on camel scene, 8" T., blue mark #52 .... $400.00 – 475.00
Plate 757
    Cookie or cracker jar, man on camel scene, 8½" T., green
    mark #47 .... $375.00 – 450.00
Plate 758
    Vase, man on camel scene, 9" T., green mark #47 .... $325.00 – 400.00

PAGES 134 and 135

All With Hunt Scene.

Plate 759
    Candy dish, 7½" L., blue mark #52 .... $225.00 – 275.00
Plate 760
    Mug, 4¾" T., green mark #47 .... $250.00 – 300.00
Plate 761
    Bon bon dish, 5½" W., green mark #47 .... $200.00 – 260.00
Plate 762
    Humidor, 7¼" T., blue mark #47 .... $650.00 – 750.00
Plate 763
    Wine jug, 9½" T., blue mark #52 .... $850.00 – 950.00
Plate 764
    Vase, 9¼" T., green mark #47 .... $375.00 – 450.00
Plate 765
    Cracker jar, 9½" W., 5" T., blue mark #52 .... $350.00 – 425.00
Plate 766
    Hanging plaque, 9½" W., green mark #47 .... $375.00 – 450.00
Plate 767
    Hanging plaque, 10" W., green mark #47 .... $325.00 – 400.00

PAGES 136 and 137

All With Woodland Scene.

Plate 768
    Chocolate set, set has pot 10¼" T., four cups and
    saucers, green mark #47 .... $900.00 – 1,100.00
Plate 769
    Compote, 6½" W., 3½" T., green mark #47 .... $250.00 – 325.00
Plate 770
    Coffee set, after-dinner, has tray 12" dia., pot 6½" T., creamer
    3" T., sugar bowl 3½" T. incl. finial, green mark #47 .... $850.00 – 1,100.00
Plate 771
    Wine jug, 9½" T., blue mark #52 .... $850.00 – 1,000.00
Plate 772
    Ewer, 6½" T., blue mark #52 .... $400.00 – 450.00
Plate 773
    Vase, 6¼" T., blue mark #52 .... $400.00 – 475.00

Plate 774
    Tea set, set has tray 12" dia., teapot 6" T., creamer,
    sugar, six cups and saucers, mark #119 .... $950.00 – 1,100.00
Plate 775
    Hanging plaque, 10" W., green mark #52 .... $350.00 – 425.00
Plate 776
    Hanging plaque, 10" W., green mark #47 .... $350.00 – 425.00
Plate 777
    Compote, small 5" W., incl, handles, green mark #47 ...... $175.00 – 225.00
Plate 778
    Salt and pepper shaker set, each 2½" T., green mark #47 $100.00 – 150.00
    Mustard pot, 2¾" T., green mark #47 .... $85.00 – 125.00

PAGES 138 and 139

Plate 779
    Humidor, 5" T., decorated w/mythological griffins (animals
    w/the body and hind legs of a lion and the head and wings
    of an eagle), blue mark #47 .... $425.00 – 500.00
Plate 780
    Humidor, 6" T., green mark #47 .... $350.00 – 425.00
    Humidor, 6¾" T., green mark #47 .... $350.00 – 425.00
    Humidor, 6" green mark #47 .... $350.00 – 425.00
Plate 781
    Humidor, 6½" T., green mark #47 .... $375.00 – 425.00
Plate 782
    Humidor, 5½" T., green mark #47 .... $450.00 – 525.00
Plate 783
    Humidor, has some moriage trim, 6" T., green mark #47 .. $575.00 – 650.00
Plate 784
    Humidor, 5½" T., green mark #47 .... $450.00 – 525.00
    Humidor, 6" T., green mark #47 .... $450.00 – 525.00
Plate 785
    Humidor, 6" T., green mark #47 .... $575.00 – 650.00
Plate 786
    Humidor, 5½" T., green mark #52 .... $450.00 – 525.00
    Humidor, 6¾" T., blue mark #52 .... $350.00 – 425.00
    Humidor, has version of hunt scene as decor, 6" T., blue
    mark #52 .... $500.00 – 600.00
Plate 787
    Humidor, 6½" T., green mark #47 .... $475.00 – 575.00

PAGES 140 and 141

Plate 788
    Humidor, 5¾" T., green mark #47 .... $275.00 – 350.00
    Ashtray, 3¼" dia., green mark #47 .... $90.00 – 130.00
Plate 789
    Humidor, 6" T., blue mark #47 .... $450.00 – 525.00
Plate 790
    Humidor, 6½" T., green mark #47 .... $550.00 – 625.00
Plate 791
    Humidor, 5" T., green mark #47 .... $300.00 – 350.00
Plate 792
    Humidor, 7" T., green mark #47 .... $800.00 – 900.00
Plate 793
    Humidor, 5½" T., green mark #47 .... $450.00 – 525.00
Plate 794
    Humidor, 4" T., green mark #47 .... $600.00 – 700.00
Plate 795
    Humidor, 7" T., green mark #47 .... $550.00 – 650.00
Plate 796
    Humidor, 7" T., blue mark #52 .... $400.00 – 500.00
Plate 797
    Humidor, 6¾" T., green mark # 47 .... $450.00 – 550.00
Plate 798
    Humidor, 7¼" T., green mark #47 .... $475.00 – 550.00

PAGES 142 and 143

Plate 799
    Humidor, 5" T., some moriage trim, green mark #47 .... $450.00 – 525.00
Plate 800
    Humidor, 7½" T., green mark #47 .... $400.00 – 500.00
Plate 801
    Ashtray, 5" W., green mark #47 .... $110.00 – 150.00
Plate 802
    Ashtray, 4¼" W., blue mark #84 .... $75.00 – 110.00

247

Plate 803

Humidor, 6½" T., green mark #47 .... $400.00 – 500.00

Plate 804

Ashtray, 4¾" L., green mark #47 .... $90.00 – 130.00

Plate 805

Humidor, 6" T., green mark #47 .... $850.00 – 1,000.00

Plate 806

Ashtray, 4½" W., green mark #47 .... $100.00 – 140.00

Ashtray, 5½" W., green mark #47 .... $100.00 – 140.00

Ashtray 4½" W., green mark #47 .... $100.00 – 140.00

Plate 807

Humidor, figural of squirrel finial, 8" T., blue mark #52 ...... $550.00 – 650.00

Plate 808

Ashtray, 5½" W., green mark #47 .... $120.00 – 160.00

Ashtray, 6" W., green mark #47 .... $100.00 – 150.00

Ashtray, 5½" W., green mark #47 .... $120.00 – 160.00

Plate 809

Ashtray, 4¾" W., green mark #47 .... $120.00 – 160.00

Ashtray, 4¾" W., green mark #47 .... $120.00 – 160.00

Ashtray, 4¾" W., green mark #47 .... $100.00 – 140.00

PAGES 144 and 145

Plate 810

Combination matchbox holder and ashtray, 3½" T., blue
mark #47 .... $175.00 – 250.00

Plate 811

Ashtray, 6¼" W., green mark #47 .... $100.00 – 140.00

Plate 812

Combination matchbox holder and ashtray, 3½" T., blue
mark #47 .... $175.00 – 250.00

Plate 813

Ashtray, 5" W., green mark #47 .... $110.00 – 140.00

Plate 814

Cigarette Box, 4½" L., green mark #47 .... $225.00 – 275.00

Plate 815

Ashtray, 5¼" W., green mark #47 .... $125.00 – 160.00

Ashtray, 5¼" W., green mark #47 .... $125.00 – 160.00

Plate 816

Ashtray, 5½" W., green mark #47 .... $135.00 – 175.00

Plate 817

Combination matchbox holder and ashtray, 3" T., green ..
mark #47 .... $160.00 – 235.00

Combination matchbox holder and ashtray, 3½" T., green
mark #47 .... $200.00 – 250.00

Plate 818

Combination matchbox holder and ashtray, 4¾" T., green
mark #47 .... $130.00 – 160.00

Plate 819

Hanging double matchbox holder, 6" L., green
mark #47 .... $135.00 – 170.00

Hanging single matchbox holder, 4½" L., green
mark #47 .... $125.00 – 160.00

Plate 820

Combination matchbox holder and ashtray, 4½" T., green
mark #47 .... $175.00 – 225.00

PAGES 146 and 147

Plate 821

Smoke set, 4-pc., tray 7¾" W., green mark #47 .... $750.00 – 850.00

Plate 822

Smoke set, 4-pc., tray 7½" W., green mark #47 .... $525.00 – 625.00

Plate 823

Smoke set, 4-pc., tray 6¾" W., green mark #47 .... $750.00 – 850.00

Plate 824

Ashtray, 4" W., green mark #47 .... $125.00 – 175.00

Plate 825

Smoke set, 6-pc., tray 11½" L., blue mark #3 .... $950.00 – 1,200.00

Plate 826

Cigar box, 5½" L., green mark #47 .... $225.00 – 275.00

Plate 827

Smoke set, 3-pc., tray 7" W., green mark #47 .... $275.00 – 350.00

Plate 828

Cigarette box, 4½" L., green mark #47 .... $225.00 – 275.00

Cigarette box, 4½" L., green mark #47 .... $225.00 – 275.00

Plate 829

Smoke set, 4-pc., tray 7" dia., green mark #47.................. $650.00 – 775.00

PAGES 148 and 149

Plate 830

Ladies' desk set, tray 8½" L. x 5¼" W., green mark #47 .... $475.00 – 575.00

Plate 831

Inkwell w/pen rest, 3½" T., green mark #47 .... $175.00 – 225.00

Plate 832

Stein, 7" T., green mark #47 .... $500.00 – 600.00

Plate 833

Stein, 7" T., green mark #47 .... $500.00 – 600.00

Plate 834

Inkwell w/tray and pen rest, tray 5½" L., green mark #47 .. $175.00 – 235.00

Plate 835

Desk set, blotter corner 4" L., ink blotter 4½" L., envelope
holder 3" T., inkwell 4" W., tray 8½" L., green mark #47 .... $650.00 – 750.00

Plate 836

Inkwell w/pen rest tray, tray 5½" L., green mark #47 .... $175.00 – 225.00

Blotter, 4½" L., green mark #47 .... $140.00 – 180.00

Plate 837

Inkwell, 3" W., green mark #47 .... $200.00 – 250.00

Plate 838

Stamp box, portrays hoo bird, 2¾" L., green mark #47 .... $90.00 – 125.00

Plate 839

Ladies' desk set, stamp box 3" L., inkwell 3½" T.,
envelope holder 4" L., blotter 4½" L., green mark #47 ...... $500.00 – 600.00

PAGES 150 and 151

Plate 840

Mug, 5½" T., green mark #47 .... $250.00 – 300.00

Plate 841

Mug, 5½" T., green mark #47 .... $225.00 – 275.00

Plate 842

Mug, 4½" T., green mark #47 .... $140.00 – 180.00

Plate 843

Mug, 5½" T., green mark #47 .... $250.00 – 300.00

Plate 844

Mug, 5½" T., green mark #47 .... $250.00 – 300.00

Mug, 5½" T., green mark #47 .... $250.00 – 300.00

Plate 845

Mug, 5" T., green mark #47 .... $250.00 – 300.00

Plate 846

Mug, 5" T., gold mark #47.................................. $300.00 – 400.00

Plate 847

Mug, 5" T., green mark #47 .... $250.00 – 300.00

Mug, 5½" T., green mark #47 .... $300.00 – 400.00

Plate 848

Tankard set, tankard 11" T., comes w/six mugs 4¾" T.,
has some moriage trim, green mark #47..........................$2,800.00 – 3,200.00

Plate 849

Stein, 7" T., green mark #47 .... $550.00 – 650.00

PAGES 152 and 153

Plate 850

Tankard, 14¾" T., green mark #26 .... $700.00 – 800.00

Plate 851

Mug, 5¾" T., green mark #47 .... $250.00 – 300.00

Plate 852

Tankard, 14½" T., green mark #52 .... $425.00 – 525.00

Plate 853

Tankard, 14" T., blue mark #52 .... $700.00 – 800.00

Plate 854

Tankard set, tankard 11" T., five mugs 4¾" T., green
mark #47 .... $2,800.00 – 3,200.00

Plate 855

Tankard set, tankard 11" T., four mugs 4¾" T., green
mark #47 .... $2,300.00 – 2,700.00

PAGES 154 and 155

Plate 856

Wine jug, 9½" T., green mark #47.................................. $850.00 – 950.00

Plate 857

Wine jug, 8¼" T., green mark #47.................................. $750.00 – 850.00

Plate 858

Whiskey jug, 8" T., blue mark #52 .... $650.00 – 750.00

Plate 859
   Wine jug, 11" T., has some moriage trim, blue mark #47 .. $850.00 – 950.00
Plate 860
   Whiskey jug, 7½" T., green mark #47 .... $700.00 – 800.00
   Whiskey jug, 7½" T., blue mark #52 .... $625.00 – 725.00
Plate 861
   Whiskey jug, 7½" T., blue mark #52 .... $625.00 – 725.00
   Whiskey jug, 7" T., green mark #52 .... $625.00 – 725.00
Plate 862
   Whiskey jug, 6½" T., green mark #47 .... $625.00 – 725.00
Plate 863
   Whiskey jug, 7½" T., green mark #47 .... $650.00 – 750.00
   Whiskey jug, 7½" T., green mark #47 .... $650.00 – 750.00
Plate 864
   Wine jug, 7¾" T., green mark #47 .... $750.00 – 850.00

PAGES 156 and 157

Plate 865
   Hanging plaque, 12" W., green mark #47 .... $425.00 – 500.00
Plate 866
   Hanging plaque, 10" W., green mark #47 .... $225.00 – 275.00
Plate 867
   Hanging plaque, 10" W., green mark #47 .... $225.00 – 275.00
Plate 868
   Hanging plaque, 10¼" W., green mark #47 .... $700.00 – 800.00
Plate 869
   Hanging plaque, 10¼" W., green mark #47 .... $700.00 – 800.00
Plate 870
   Hanging plaque, 12" W., artist signed, green mark #47 .... $425.00 – 500.00
Plate 871
   Hanging plaque, 11" W., green mark #47 .... $250.00 – 300.00
Plate 872
   Hanging plaque, 10" W., green mark #47 .... $250.00 – 300.00
Plate 873
   Hanging plaque, 12" W., green mark #47 .... $425.00 – 500.00

PAGES 158 and 159

Plate 874
   Hanging plaque, 9" W., green mark #47 .... $275.00 – 325.00
Plate 875
   Hanging plaque, 9" W., green mark #47 .... $275.00 – 325.00
Plate 876
   Hanging plaque, 10" W., blue mark #52 .... $850.00 – 1,000.00
Plate 877
   Hanging plaque, 10" W., blue mark #52 .... $300.00 – 350.00
Plate 878
   Hanging plaque, 11" W., green mark #47 .... $425.00 – 500.00
Plate 879
   Hanging plaque, 7¾" W., blue mark #52 .... $375.00 – 450.00
Plate 880
   Hanging plaque, 8½" W., blue mark #52 .... $425.00 – 500.00
Plate 881
   Hanging plaque, 10" W., blue mark #52 .... $425.00 – 500.00
Plate 882
   Hanging plaque, 11" W., green mark #47 .... $350.00 – 425.00
Plate 883
   Hanging plaque, 10" W., green mark #47 .... $325.00 – 400.00
Plate 884
   Hanging plaque, 11" W., blue mark #52 .... $275.00 – 300.00
   Hanging plaque, 10" W., green mark #47 .... $300.00 – 375.00

PAGES 160 and 161

Plate 885
   Hanging plaque, 10" W., green mark #47 .... $250.00 – 300.00
Plate 886
   Hanging plaque, 10" W., green mark #47 .... $275.00 – 325.00
Plate 887
   Hanging plaque, 10" W., green mark #47 .... $250.00 – 300.00
Plate 888
   Hanging plaque, 7½" W., some moriage trim, green mark
   #47 .... $150.00 – 200.00
Plate 889
   Hanging plaque, 11" W., green mark #47 .... $350.00 – 425.00
Plate 890
   Hanging plaque, 8¾" W., green mark #47 .... $250.00 – 300.00

Plate 891
   Hanging plaque, 10" W., green mark #47 .... $225.00 – 275.00
   Hanging plaque, 10" W., green mark #47 .... $250.00 – 300.00
Plate 892
   Hanging plaque, 9" W., green mark #47 .... $250.00 – 300.00
Plate 893
   Hanging plaque, 10" W., green mark #47 .... $300.00 – 375.00
   Hanging plaque, 10" W., green mark #47 .... $300.00 – 375.00
Plate 894
   Hanging plaque, 10" W., blue mark #52 .... $300.00 – 375.00

PAGES 162 and 163

Plate 895
   Hanging plaque, 10" W., green mark #47 .... $225.00 – 275.00
Plate 896
   Hanging plaque, 10" W., green mark #47 .... $225.00 – 275.00
Plate 897
   Hanging plaque, 10" W., green mark #47 .... $225.00 – 275.00
Plate 898
   Hanging plaque, 10" W., green mark #47 .... $225.00 – 275.00
Plate 899
   Hanging plaque, 7¾" W., green mark #47 .... $300.00 – 375.00
Plate 900
   Hanging plaque, 7½" W., green mark #47 .... $275.00 – 325.00
Plate 901
   Hanging plaque, 7¾" W., green mark #47 .... $300.00 – 375.00
Plate 902
   Hanging plaque, 10" W., green mark #47 .... $250.00 – 300.00
Plate 903
   Hanging plaque, 7½" W., blue mark #47 .... $200.00 – 250.00
   Hanging plaque, 7½" W., green mark #47 .... $200.00 – 250.00
Plate 904
   Hanging plaque, 9½" W., green mark #47 .... $400.00 – 500.00

PAGES 164 and 165

Plate 905
   Hanging plaque, 10" W., green mark #47 .... $225.00 – 275.00
Plate 906
   Hanging plaque, 10" W., green mark #47 .... $225.00 – 275.00
Plate 907
   Hanging plaque, 10" W., green mark #47 .... $225.00 – 275.00
Plate 908
   Hanging plaque, 10" W., green mark #47 .... $225.00 – 275.00
Plate 909
   Hanging plaque, 10" W., green mark #47 .... $225.00 – 275.00
Plate 910
   Hanging plaque, 10" W., green mark #47 .... $250.00 – 300.00
Plate 911
   Hanging plaque, 7¾" W., blue mark #52 .... $175.00 – 225.00
Plate 912
   Hanging plaque, 10" W., green mark #47 .... $225.00 – 275.00
Plate 913
   Hanging plaque, 10" W., green mark #47 .... $225.00 – 275.00
Plate 914
   Hanging plaque, 10" W., green mark #47 .... $225.00 – 275.00

PAGES 166 and 167

Plate 915
   Hanging plaque, 11" W., some moriage trim, green mark
   #47 .... $225.00 – 275.00
Plate 916
   Hanging plaque, 10" W., green mark #47 .... $225.00 – 275.00
Plate 917
   Hanging plaque, 10" W., green mark #47 .... $225.00 – 275.00
Plate 918
   Hanging plaque, 11" W., green mark #47 .... $325.00 – 400.00
   Hanging plaque, 10" W., green mark #47 .... $225.00 – 275.00
Plate 919
   Hanging plaque, 10" W., green mark #47 .... $225.00 – 275.00
Plate 920
   Hanging plaque, 9" W., green mark #47 .... $225.00 – 275.00
Plate 921
   Hanging plaque, 10½" W., green mark #47 .... $225.00 – 275.00
Plate 922
   Hanging plaque, 10" W., green mark #47 .... $225.00 – 275.00

Hanging plaque, 11" W., green mark #47 .... $275.00 – 325.00
Plate 923
    Hanging plaque, 10" W., green mark #47 .... $250.00 – 300.00

PAGES 168 and 169

Plate 924
    Hanging plaque, 9" W., green mark #47 .... $200.00 – 250.00
Plate 925
    Hanging plaque, 10" W., green mark #47 .... $225.00 – 275.00
Plate 926
    Hanging plaque, 10" W., green mark #47 .... $250.00 – 300.00
Plate 927
    Hanging plaque, 10" W., green mark #47 .... $250.00 – 300.00
Plate 928
    Hanging plaque, 10" W., green mark #47 .... $225.00 – 275.00
Plate 929
    Hanging plaque, 6" W., green mark #47 .... $225.00 – 275.00
Plate 930
    Hanging plaque, 11" W., green mark #47 .... $425.00 – 500.00
Plate 931
    Hanging plaque, 9¼" W., blue mark #52 .... $225.00 – 275.00
Plate 932
    Hanging plaque, 11" W., blue mark #47 .... $250.00 – 300.00
Plate 933
    Hanging plaque, 10" W., green mark #47 .... $300.00 – 375.00
Plate 934
    Hanging plaque, 9" W., green mark #47 .... $225.00 – 275.00

PAGES 170 and 171

Plate 935
    Vase, 10" T., blue mark #52 .... $325.00 – 400.00
Plate 936
    Vase, 12" T., blue mark #52 .... $400.00 – 500.00
Plate 937
    Vase, 9" T., green mark #47 .... $250.00 – 300.00
Plate 938
    Vase, 9½" T., green mark #47 .... $300.00 – 375.00
Plate 939
    Vase, 10½" T., green mark #47 .... $300.00 – 375.00
Plate 940
    Vase, 12¾" T., blue mark #52 .... $325.00 – 400.00
Plate 941
    Vase, 13" T., blue mark #52 .... $400.00 – 500.00
Plate 942
    Vase, 8½" T., blue mark #47 .... $250.00 – 300.00
Plate 943
    Vase, 9½" T., green mark #47 .... $300.00 – 375.00
Plate 944
    Vase, 10½" T., blue mark #52 .... $300.00 – 375.00

PAGES 172 and 173

Plate 945
    Vase, 8½" T., green mark #52 .... $275.00 – 325.00
    Vase, 6¼" T., green mark #47 .... $175.00 – 225.00
Plate 946
    Vase, 10½" T., blue mark #52 .... $300.00 – 375.00
Plate 947
    Vase, 16½" T., blue mark #52 .... $600.00 – 750.00
Plate 948
    Vase, 6¼" T., man on camel scene, green mark #47 .... $275.00 – 325.00
    Vase, 8" T., green mark #47 .... $150.00 – 200.00
Plate 949
    Vase, 15" T., green mark #52 .... $400.00 – 500.00
Plate 950
    Vase, 8½" T., green mark #47 .... $250.00 – 300.00
    Vase, 8½" T., green mark #47 .... $250.00 – 300.00
Plate 951
    Vases, 10¾" T., blue mark #52 ....(Each) $325.00 – 400.00
Plate 952
    Vase, 13½" T., green mark #47 .... $300.00 – 400.00
    Vase, 13½" T., same as first, diff. decoration., green mark #47 $300.00 – 400.00
Plate 953
    Vase, 10½" T., green mark #52 .... $275.00 – 325.00
Plate 954
    Vase, 13" T., blue mark #47 .... $350.00 – 425.00

PAGES 174 and 175

Plate 955
    Vase, 7½" T., green mark #47 .... $150.00 – 200.00
    Vase, 7¼" T., green mark #47 .... $150.00 – 200.00
Plate 956
    Vases, 7¾" T., green mark #47 ....(Each) $200.00 – 275.00
Plate 957
    Vase, 8" T., green mark #47 .... $225.00 – 275.00
Plate 958
    Vases, some moriage trim, each 9" T., blue mark
    #52 ....(Each) $275.00 – 325.00
Plate 959
    Vase, 8" T., some moriage trim, blue mark #52 .... $275.00 – 325.00
Plate 960
    Basket vase, 6" T., 7¼" W., green mark #47 .... $225.00 – 275.00
Plate 961
    Vase, 7½" T., blue mark #52 .... $300.00 – 375.00
Plate 962
    Ewer, 6¾" T., blue mark #52 .... $200.00 – 275.00
Plate 963
    Ewer, 12½" T., blue mark #52 .... $450.00 – 525.00
Plate 964
    Vase, 10¾" T., green mark #52 .... $325.00 – 400.00
Plate 965
    Vase, 13" T., blue mark #47 .... $300.00 – 400.00
Plate 966
    Vase, 8" T., blue mark #52 .... $275.00 – 350.00

PAGES 176 and 177

Plate 967
    Vase, 10½" T., green mark #47 .... $175.00 – 250.00
Plate 968
    Vase, 6½" T., green mark #47 .... $100.00 – 150.00
    Vase, 6½" T., green mark #47 .... $100.00 – 150.00
Plate 969
    Vases, 9" T., green mark #47.............................(Each) $200.00 – 275.00
Plate 970
    Vase, 9" T., blue mark #52 .... $300.00 – 375.00
Plate 971
    Vase, 9½" T., green mark #47 .... $175.00 – 225.00
    Vase, 8" T., green mark #47 .... $150.00 – 200.00
Plate 972
    Vase, 10" T., green mark #52 .... $325.00 – 400.00
    Vase, 10¼" T., blue mark #52......................... $325.00 – 400.00
Plate 973
    Vase, 8" T., blue mark #52 .... $275.00 – 350.00
Plate 974
    Ewer, 13" T., blue mark #52 .... $500.00 – 600.00
Plate 975
    Vase, 11¼" T., green mark #52 .... $325.00 – 400.00

PAGES 178 and 179

Plate 976
    Vase, 13" T., green mark #47 .... $400.00 – 500.00
Plate 977
    Vase, 8¾" T., green mark #47 .... $200.00 – 250.00
Plate 978
    Vase, 11½" T., green mark #47 .... $300.00 – 375.00
Plate 979
    Vase, 13½" T., green mark #47 .... $800.00 – 950.00
    Vase, 13¾" T., green mark #47 .... $800.00 – 950.00
Plate 980
    Vases, 14" T., green mark #47.............................(Each) $400.00 – 500.00
Plate 981
    Vase, 13¾" T., green mark #47 .... $800.00 – 950.00
    Vase, 13" T., green mark #47 .... $800.00 – 950.00
Plate 982
    Vase, 7" T., green mark #47 .... $100.00 – 150.00
    Vase, 8" T., gold overlay, man on camel scene, green
    mark #47......................... $325.00 – 400.00
Plate 983
    Vase, 8½" T., green mark #47 .... $350.00 – 425.00
    Vase, 8¼" T., green mark #47 .... $350.00 – 425.00
Plate 984
    Vase, 10½" T., green mark #47 .... $300.00 – 375.00
    Vase, 10½" T., green mark #47 .... $300.00 – 375.00

PAGES 180 and 181

Plate 985
  Vase, 11" T., green mark #47 .... $325.00 – 400.00
Plate 986
  Vase, 9½" T., green mark #47 .... $300.00 – 375.00
Plate 987
  Vase, 8½" T., green mark #47 .... $200.00 – 250.00
Plate 988
  Urns, ea. 2-pcs. bolted together, 8¼" T., green mark #47 ..(ea.) $275.00 – 325.00
Plate 989
  Vase, 6" T., blue mark #38 .... $135.00 – 175.00
  Bon bon dish, 5" W., blue mark #38 .... $125.00 – 175.00
  Vase, 7" T., blue mark #38 .... $135.00 – 175.00
Plate 990
  Vase, 13" T., green mark #47 .... $700.00 – 800.00
Plate 991
  Vase, 13" T., unmarked .... $600.00 – 700.00
Plate 992
  Vase, 7" T., green mark #47 .... $250.00 – 300.00
Plate 993
  Vase, 10" blue mark #47 .... $350.00 – 425.00
  Vase, 9½" T., blue mark #52 .... $350.00 – 425.00
Plate 994
  Vase, 15" T., green mark #47 .... $900.00 – 1,100.00
Plate 995
  Vase, 6¾" T., blue mark #38 .... $300.00 – 400.00
  Vase, 6¾" T., pattern stamped, green mark #47 .... $275.00 – 350.00

PAGES 182 and 183

Plate 996
  Vase, 9½" T., reverse side of plate #1002, mark #91 .... $225.00 – 275.00
Plate 997
  Vases, 10¼" T., unmarked ....(Each) $200.00 – 275.00
Plate 998
  Vase, 12" T., green mark #47 .... $325.00 – 400.00
Plate 999
  Vase, 12½" T., green mark #47 .... $425.00 – 525.00
Plate 1000
  Vase, 8" T., blue mark #52 .... $275.00 – 325.00
Plate 1001
  Vase, 8½" T., blue mark #47 .... $300.00 – 375.00
Plate 1002
  Vase, 9½" T., mark #91, see reverse side in plate #996.... $225.00 – 275.00
Plate 1003
  Vase, 8" T., blue mark #52 .... $325.00 – 400.00
Plate 1004
  Vase, 14" T., green mark #47 .... $800.00 – 950.00
Plate 1005
  Ewer, 12¼" T., blue mark #52.. $500.00 – 600.00

PAGES 184 and 185

Plate 1006
  Vase, 6½" T., green mark #47 .... $175.00 – 235.00
Plate 1007
  Vase, 10" T., blue mark #17 .... $275.00 – 350.00
Plate 1008
  Vase, 13" T., green mark #47 .... $400.00 – 500.00
Plate 1009
  Vase, 3" T., green mark #47 .... $125.00 – 160.00
  Vase, 4½" T., green mark #47 .... $70.00 – 100.00
  Vase, 2½" T., green mark #47 .... $40.00 – 65.00
  Vase, 2½" T., green mark #47 .... $40.00 – 65.00
Plate 1010
  Vase, 12" T., blue mark #52 .... $400.00 – 500.00
  Vase, 10" T., blue mark #52 .... $300.00 – 375.00
Plate 1011
  Vase, 7½" T., green mark #47 .... $300.00 – 375.00
Plate 1012
  Vase, 10" T., green mark #47 .... $325.00 – 400.00
  Vase, 11" T., blue mark #47 .... $325.00 – 400.00
Plate 1013
  Vase, 13" T., green mark #47 .... $400.00 – 500.00
Plate 1014
  Vase, 10¼" T., blue mark #47 .... $300.00 – 375.00
Plate 1015
  Vase, 12" T., blue mark #52 .... $400.00 – 500.00

Plate 1016
  Vase, 9¾" T., green mark #47 .... $300.00 – 375.00
  Vase, 8¾" T., green mark #47 .... $275.00 – 350.00
Plate 1017
  Vase, 7½" T., blue mark #47 .... $275.00 – 350.00
  Vase, 8½" T., blue mark #47 .... $275.00 – 300.00

PAGES 186 and 187

Plate 1018
  Vase, 8" T., green mark #47 .... $200.00 – 275.00
Plate 1019
  Vase, 9½" T., blue mark #52.. $300.00 – 375.00
Plate 1020
  Vase, 9¼" T., green mark #47 .... $175.00 – 225.00
Plate 1021
  Vase 6" T., blue mark #52 .... $200.00 – 275.00
  Vase 6" T., blue mark #47 .... $200.00 – 275.00
Plate 1022
  Vase, 14" T., green mark #47 .... $800.00 – 1,000.00
Plate 1023
  Vase, 12" T., green mark #47 .... $400.00 – 500.00
Plate 1024
  Vase, 14" T., green mark #47 .... $500.00 – 600.00
Plate 1025
  Vase, 13" T., green mark #47 .... $850.00 – 1,100.00
Plate 1026
  Vases, each 13" T., green mark #47 ....(Each) $350.00 – 425.00

PAGES 188 and 189

Plate 1027
  Vase, 9¾" T., green mark #47 .... $225.00 – 300.00
Plate 1028
  Vases, 7¼" T., mark #55 ....(Each) $150.00 – 200.00
Plate 1029
  Vase, 10" T., blue mark #52 .... $200.00 – 250.00
Plate 1030
  Vase, 10" T., green mark #52 .... $225.00 – 300.00
Plate 1031
  Covered urn, 13" T., green mark #52 .... $800.00 – 950.00
Plate 1032
  Vase, 11" T., blue mark #47 .... $325.00 – 400.00
Plate 1033
  Vase, 5¾" T., green mark #47 .... $300.00 – 375.00
Plate 1034
  Vase, 7¼" T., green mark #47 .... $225.00 – 275.00
Plate 1035
  Vase, 6½" T., green mark #47 .... $250.00 – 300.00

PAGES 190 and 191

Plate 1036
  Covered urn, 9" T., blue mark #52 .... $650.00 – 750.00
Plate 1037
  Covered urn, 11" T., mark #89 .... $550.00 – 650.00
Plate 1038
  Large urn, 24½" T., blue mark #52 ....$4,500.00 – 5,500.00
Plate 1039
  Large urn, 20¾" T., blue mark #52 .... $3,000.00 – 3,400.00
Plate 1040
  Covered urn, 14" T., blue mark #52 .... $1,200.00 – 1,400.00
Plate 1041
  Urn, 12" T., green mark #47 .... $700.00 – 900.00
Plate 1042
  Urn, 15" T., blue mark #47 .... $1,200.00 – 1,400.00
Plate 1043
  Covered urn, 14¼" T., green mark #47 .... $1,400.00 – 1,800.00

PAGES 192 and 193

Plate 1044
  Column ferner, 5" T., green mark #47 .... $300.00 – 400.00
Plate 1045
  Ferner, 8½" W., w/relief molded hndls., 3¾" T., grn. mark #47 .. $275.00 – 325.00
Plate 1046
  Ferner, 6¾" W., green mark #47....................................... $225.00 – 275.00

Plate 1047
    Hanging pot, 5" T., 4" W., blue mark #47 .... $375.00 – 450.00
Plate 1048
    Hanging pot, 5" T., 4" W., green mark #47 .... $375.00 – 450.00
Plate 1049
    Ferner, 9½" L., green mark #47 .... $275.00 – 325.00
    Ferner, 7½" L., green mark #47 .... $200.00 – 250.00
Plate 1050
    Ferner, 8" L., green mark #47 .... $300.00 – 400.00
    Ferner, 6¾" L., green mark #47 .... $225.00 – 275.00
Plate 1051
    Hanging pot, 5" T., green mark #47 .... $325.00 – 400.00
Plate 1052
    Hanging pot, 5" T., green mark #47 .... $375.00 – 450.00
    Hanging pot, 5" T., green mark #47 .... $325.00 – 400.00
Plate 1053
    Hanging pot, 5" T., green mark #47 .... $325.00 – 400.00

PAGES 194 and 195

Plate 1054
    Cookie or cracker jar, 7" T., green mark #47 .... $225.00 – 275.00
Plate 1055
    Cookie or cracker jar, 8¼" T., green mark #52 .... $425.00 – 500.00
Plate 1056
    Ferner, 8½" W. incl. relief molded handles, green mark
    #47 .... $350.00 – 450.00
Plate 1057
    Ferner, 6" W., 3¼" T., green mark #47 .... $250.00 – 325.00
Plate 1058
    Ferner, 8½" W., incl. relief molded handles, green mark
    #47 .... $275.00 – 350.00
Plate 1059
    Cookie or cracker jar, 8½" T., green mark #47 .... $425.00 – 500.00
Plate 1060
    Cracker jar, 8" W., 6" T., green mark #47 .... $225.00 – 275.00
Plate 1061
    Cookie or cracker jar, 7½" T., green mark #52 .... $425.00 – 500.00
Plate 1062
    Cookie or cracker jar, 8½" T., green mark #47 .... $375.00 – 450.00
Plate 1063
    Cookie or cracker jar, 7" T., green mark #47 .... $350.00 – 425.00

PAGES 196 and 197

Plate 1064
    Cracker jar, 7" W., mark #80.......................... $180.00 – 250.00
    Cracker jar, 7" W., blue mark #52.................... $225.00 – 275.00
Plate 1065
    Cracker or cookie jar, 7" T., blue mark #52 ...... $350.00 – 450.00
Plate 1066
    Punch set, punch bowl 16" W. incl. handles, cups 4" T.,
    green mark #47.. $1,200.00 – 1,400.00
Plate 1067
    Punch set, punch bowl 9½" W., cups 3¾" T., green mark
    #47 .... $950.00 – 1,150.00

PAGES 198 and 199

Plate 1068
    Game platter and sauce dish, (see plates #1069, 1072 and
    1073 for rest of set), platter 17" L., sauce dish 6½" L.,
    all green mark #47 .... $1,800.00 – 2,200.00
Plate 1069
    Two game plates, matching #1068, each 8½" W., green
    mark #47 ....(Set) $1,800.00 – 2,200.00
Plate 1070
    Game set, has 16½" platter, six plates, green mark #47 .... $2,000.00 – 2,400.00
Plate 1071
    Fish set, set has 17½" platter, five plates 9" L., green
    mark #24 .... $800.00 – 950.00

PAGES 200 and 201

Plate 1072
    Game plates, match platter in plate #1068, each 8½" W.,
    green mark #47 ....(Set) $1,800.00 – 2,200.00

Plate 1073
    Game plates, match platter in plate #1068, each 8½" W.,
    green mark #47 ....(Set) $1,800.00 – 2,200.00
Plate 1074
    Game platter, 17" L., green mark #47..................... $700.00 – 850.00
Plate 1075
    After dinner coffee set, set has 9" pot, four cups and
    saucers, blue mark #52 .... $500.00 – 600.00
Plate 1076
    Chocolate set, set has 8¾" pot, four cups and saucers,
    mark #80 .... $550.00 – 650.00
Plate 1077
    Chocolate set, set has 11" T. pot, four cups and saucers,
    cups 3" T., blue mark #52 .... $600.00 – 700.00
Plate 1078
    Chocolate pot, 10¼" T., blue mark #52.............................. $375.00 – 450.00

PAGES 202 and 203

Plate 1079
    Chocolate set, set has chocolate pot, 9" T., and six cups
    and saucers, green mark #47 .... $450.00 – 525.00
Plate 1080
    Chocolate set, set has chocolate pot 10¾" T., four cups
    and saucers, mark #80 .... $450.00 – 525.00
Plate 1081
    Chocolate set, set has chocolate pot, 10¼" T., and six
    cups and saucers blue mark #52 .... $450.00 – 525.00
Plate 1082
    Chocolate set, set has chocolate pot 10" T., six cups and
    saucers, green mark #47 .... $325.00 – 375.00
Plate 1083
    Chocolate set, set has chocolate pot 9½" T., four cups
    and saucers, green mark #81 .... $450.00 – 550.00
Plate 1084
    Chocolate pot, 9¾" T., blue mark #52 .... $300.00 – 350.00
Plate 1085
    Chocolate set, chocolate pot 9" T., four cups and saucers,
    green mark #79.................................... $350.00 – 425.00
Plate 1086
    Chocolate set, pot 9½" T., four cups and saucers blue
    mark #52 .... $600.00 – 725.00
Plate 1087
    Coffee set, after-dinner, pot 9" T., six cups and saucers,
    all pieces have heavy gold dragon motif, green mark #47 $550.00 – 650.00
Plate 1088
    Chocolate pot, 9¾" T., blue mark #52 .... $225.00 – 275.00

PAGES 204 and 205

Plate 1089
    After dinner coffee set, pot 6½" T., set incl. four cups and
    saucers, copper saucers are incised "NANNING QUALITY /
    BOWNAN / MERIDAN CONN. 163", red mark #47 .... $275.00 – 350.00
Plate 1090
    Three piece tea set, pot 6½" T., green mark #47 .... $200.00 – 250.00
Plate 1091
    Chocolate set, pot 10½" T., six cups and saucers green
    mark #47.. $1,100.00 – 1,300.00
Plate 1092
    Chocolate set, pot 10" T., four cups and saucers, blue
    mark #52.. $1,100.00 – 1,300.00

PAGES 206 and 207

Plate 1093
    Chocolate pot, 9½" T., mark #47...................... $100.00 – 140.00
    Chocolate pot, 9¾" T., blue mark #38 .... $100.00 – 140.00
    Chocolate pot, 8½" T., blue mark #52............... $120.00 – 160.00
Plate 1094
    Coffee set, after-dinner, pot 6½" T., five cups and
    saucers, green mark #81 .... $425.00 – 500.00
Plate 1095
    Coffee set, after-dinner, pot 8" T., tray 12" W., set incl.
    six cups and saucers, green mark #47 .... $1,000.00 – 1,200.00
Plate 1096
    Chocolate set, pot 9¾" T., four cups and saucers green
    mark #52 .... $725.00 – 900.00

Plate 1097
    Tea set, set has teapot, creamer, sugar and four cups and
    saucers, pot 5" T., blue mark #52 .... $350.00 – 425.00
Plate 1098
    Tea set, set has teapot, creamer, sugar and six cups and
    saucers, pot 4" T., blue mark #52 .... $350.00 – 425.00
Plate 1099
    Coffee set, after-dinner, set has pot, five cups and saucers,
    salt and pepper shakers, mark #109 .... $375.00 – 450.00
Plate 1100
    Chocolate set, set has pot 9½" T., four cups and saucers,
    blue mark #84 .... $250.00 – 325.00
    Matching cake plate, 10½" W., blue mark #84 .... $75.00 – 100.00
    Matching cookie or cracker jar, 8" W., blue #84 .... $150.00 – 200.00

Plate 1101
    Three-piece tea set, pot 5½" T., blue mark #52 .... $250.00 – 300.00
Plate 1102
    Chocolate pot, 12¼" T., blue mark #52 .... $300.00 – 375.00
Plate 1103
    Tea set, set has teapot, creamer, sugar, six cups and
    saucers, pot 6½" T., mark #71 .... $350.00 – 450.00
Plate 1104
    Tea set, set has teapot, creamer, sugar, six cups and
    saucers, blue mark #52 .... $325.00 – 425.00
    Matching 5" covered milk pitcher, green mark #47 .... $175.00 – 250.00
    Matching salt and pepper shakers, blue mark #52 .... $35.00 – 50.00
Plate 1105
    Tea set, set has teapot, creamer, sugar, four cups and
    saucers, green mark #47 .... $350.00 – 425.00
    Matching 9" vase, blue mark #52 .... $275.00 – 350.00
    Matching salt and pepper shakers, unmarked .... $40.00 – 50.00

Plate 1106
    Tea set, set has teapot, creamer and sugar, six cups and
    saucers, pot 6½" T., incl. finial, mark #71 .... $250.00 – 300.00
Plate 1107
    Tea set, set has teapot, creamer and sugar, eight cups
    and saucers, pot 5½" T., green mark #47 .... $165.00 – 230.00
Plate 1108
    Three-piece tea set, pot 5" T., mark #106 .... $135.00 – 175.00
Plate 1109
    Tea set, set has teapot, creamer and sugar, six cups and
    saucers, pot 5½" T., blue mark #52 .... $525.00 – 600.00
Plate 1110
    Tea set, set has teapot, creamer and sugar, six cups and
    saucers, pot 5¼" T., mark #73 .... $350.00 – 425.00

Plate 1111
    Tea set, set has teapot, creamer, sugar, six cups and
    saucers, pot 5¼" T., blue mark #71 .... $300.00 – 400.00
Plate 1112
    Three-piece tea set, pot 6¾" T., sugar 5", creamer 4½",
    blue mark #32 .... $225.00 – 275.00
Plate 1113
    Cake plate, 11½" W. incl. handles, green mark #52 .... $200.00 – 250.00
    Cake plate, 10" W., blue mark #52 .... $300.00 – 350.00
Plate 1114
    Chocolate pot, 10" T., blue mark #52 .... $325.00 – 400.00
Plate 1115
    Tea set, set has teapot, creamer, sugar, six cups and
    saucers, pot 6" T., green mark #47 .... $325.00 – 425.00
Plate 1116
    Chocolate pot, 10½" T., blue mark #52 .... $350.00 – 425.00
Plate 1117
    Three-piece tea set, some moriage trim, pot 4" T., green
    mark #47 .... $225.00 – 275.00
Plate 1118
    Cake set, large plate 11" dia., small plates are 6", blue
    mark #52 .... $450.00 – 550.00

Plate 1119
    Cake set, large plate 10½" dia., six small plates, each
    5¾" W., mark #81 .... $275.00 – 325.00

Plate 1120
    Cake set, large plate 11" W. plus six smaller plates, green
    mark #47 .... $200.00 – 275.00
Plate 1121
    Cake set, large plate 11" W. plus six smaller plates, green
    mark #47 .... $175.00 – 225.00
Plate 1122
    Cake set, large plate 10½" W., plus six smaller plates,
    mark #87 .... $175.00 – 225.00
Plate 1123
    Lemonade set, set has pitcher 6¼" T., six cups, green
    mark #113 .... $225.00 – 300.00
Plate 1124
    Bowl, 9" W., green mark #47 .... $100.00 – 135.00
Plate 1125
    Peanut set, master bowl 8½" L., six smaller dishes 3½"
    L., green mark #47 .... $150.00 – 200.00
Plate 1126
    Five-piece set in lacquered box, blue mark #52 .... $125.00 – 160.00
Plate 1127
    Celery set, set has 13½" L., celery dish, six salts 3¾" L.,
    green mark #47 .... $150.00 – 200.00
Plate 1128
    Large fruit compote, 12" W. incl. handles, blue mark #52 .. $300.00 – 375.00

Plate 1129
    Bowl set, large bowl 9½" W., six small bowls 5" W., blue
    mark #52 .... $225.00 – 275.00
Plate 1130
    Nut set, large bowl 8¾" W., four small bowls 3¾" W.,
    green mark #47 .... $150.00 – 200.00
Plate 1131
    Nut set, large bowl 7½" W., five small bowls 3¼" W.,
    green mark #52 .... $250.00 – 300.00
Plate 1132
    Bowl, 11" W. incl. handles, mark #89 .... $250.00 – 300.00
Plate 1133
    Bowl, 8¼" W., green mark #47 .... $200.00 – 300.00
Plate 1134
    Bowl, 6½" W., green mark #47 .... $200.00 – 300.00
Plate 1135
    Nut set, large bowl 7½" W., six small cups 3" W., green
    mark #47 .... $175.00 – 225.00
Plate 1136
    Fruit bowl, 2-pc., on pedestal, could be used as a punch
    bowl, 5¼" T., green mark #47 .... $400.00 – 500.00
Plate 1137
    Nut set, lg. bowl 7½" W., 6 sm. bowls 3" W., green mark #47.. $175.00 – 225.00
Plate 1138
    Bowl, 8½" diameter, green mark #47 .... $200.00 – 250.00

Plate 1139
    Bowl, 8½" W., green mark #47 .... $85.00 – 115.00
    Bowl, 9" W., green mark #47 .... $85.00 – 115.00
Plate 1140
    Bowl, 10½" W., mark #39 .... $200.00 – 260.00
Plate 1141
    Bowl, 9" W., green mark #47 .... $85.00 – 115.00
Plate 1142
    Bowl, 7½" W., green mark #47 .... $90.00 – 120.00
Plate 1143
    Bowl, 8" W., green mark #47 .... $75.00 – 100.00
Plate 1144
    Bowl, 9" W., green mark #47 .... $150.00 – 220.00
Plate 1145
    Candlesticks, 9½" T., blue mark #52 ....(Pair) $400.00 – 500.00
Plate 1146
    Candlesticks, 8½" T., green mark #47 ....(Pair) $325.00 – 400.00

Plate 1147
    Candlesticks, 8¼" T., green mark #47 ....(Pair) $325.00 – 400.00
    Matching ashtray, 4¾" L., green mark #47 .... $85.00 – 115.00
Plate 1148
    Candlesticks, 6¼" T., green mark #47 ....(Pair) $225.00 – 300.00
Plate 1149
    Candlestick, 6¼" T., green mark #47 .... $125.00 – 150.00
    Candlestick, 6¼" T., same mold, different decoration,
    green mark #47... $125.00 – 150.00

PAGES 222 and 223

Plate 1150
    Bowl, 10½" dia. blue mark #52 .... $200.00 – 250.00
Plate 1151
    Nut set, large 7½" dia. bowl on pedestal, six small cups,
    green mark #47 .... $200.00 – 250.00
Plate 1152
    Bowl, 8½" W., green mark #47 .... $125.00 – 160.00
Plate 1153
    Candlesticks, 8½" T., green mark #47 ....(Pair) $400.00 – 500.00
    Box without top, 6" L., green mark #47............................ $250.00 – 325.00
Plate 1154
    Candlestick, 8¼" T., blue mark #47 .... $150.00 – 200.00
Plate 1155
    Dresser set, set has tray 11" L., hatpin holder, 5" T., pin
    dish 5" W., hair receiver, 3" T. and perfume bottle, 5" T.,
    green mark #47... $500.00 – 600.00
Plate 1156
    Vanity organizer (combination stickpin holder-hatpin
    holder-ring tree) tray 7" L., blue mark #52 .... $250.00 – 300.00
    Hanging wall vase, 7" L., blue mark #52.......................... $200.00 – 275.00
Plate 1157
    Candlestick, 8" T., blue mark #47 .... $250.00 – 300.00
Plate 1158
    Heart-shaped trinket box, 4" W., blue mark #52 .... $85.00 – 120.00
    Ring holder, 3½" T., blue mark #52................................. $85.00 – 120.00
Plate 1159
    Dresser set, tray 11" L., hatpin holder 4½" T., green mark
    #47 .... $400.00 – 500.00

PAGES 224 and 225

Plate 1160
    Nut bowl, 7½" W., green mark #47 .... $75.00 – 100.00
Plate 1161
    Powder box, 4" W., green mark #47 .... $35.00 – 50.00
Plate 1162
    Talcum powder flask, 5" T., blue mark #68...................... $140.00 – 180.00
Plate 1163
    Nut set, large bowl, 7¼" dia., six small cups, 3" dia.,
    green mark #47 .... $175.00 – 250.00
Plate 1164
    Hairpin holder, 3" T., green mark #47.............................. $100.00 – 140.00
Plate 1165
    Bowl, 6" W., green mark #47 .... $100.00 – 140.00
Plate 1166
    Dresser set, tray 11" long, mark #103 .... $250.00 – 300.00
Plate 1167
    Hatpin holders, all open top
    1. 4¾" T., mark #68 .... $70.00 – 100.00
    2. 4¾" T., blue mark #52 .... $75.00 – 110.00
    3. 4¾" T., mark #7 .... $70.00 – 100.00
    4. 4⅞" T., mark #84 .... $70.00 – 100.00
    5. 4⅞" T., blue mark #52.. $75.00 – 110.00
Plate 1168
    Hatpin holders
    1. 4¾" T., green mark #47 .... $70.00 – 100.00
    2. 4¾" T., mark #84 .... $75.00 – 110.00
    3. 4¾" T., green mark #47 .... $70.00 – 100.00
    4. 4¾" T., red mark #47 .... $70.00 – 100.00
    5. 4¾" T., mark #103 .... $70.00 – 100.00
Plate 1169
    Bowl, 6" W., green mark #47 .... $65.00 – 90.00
Plate 1170
    Hatpin holders
    1. 4¾" T., holes in top, blue mark #47 .... $70.00 – 100.00
    2. 4⅝" T., open top, green mark #47 .... $70.00 – 100.00
    3. 4¾" T., open top, green mark #47 .... $70.00 – 100.00

4. 4⅝" T., open top, green mark #47 .... $70.00 – 100.00
5. 4¾" T., open top, green mark #47 .... $70.00 – 100.00

PAGES 226 and 227

Plate 1171
    Cruet, 7¼" T., green mark #47 .... $250.00 – 325.00
Plate 1172
    Feeding boat, 8" long, 2½" T., mark #55......................... $75.00 – 125.00
Plate 1173
    Butter dish, two-pc., bottom plate 7¾" dia., green mark #47 .. $125.00 – 160.00
Plate 1174
    Double sugar cube holder, 5¾" L., incl. handles, green
    mark #47.. $100.00 – 140.00
Plate 1175
    Sugar shaker, 4¾" T., mark #17 .... $100.00 – 140.00
    Sugar shaker, 3½" T., green mark #47 .... $100.00 – 140.00
Plate 1176
    Sugar shaker, 5" T., green mark #47 .... $110.00 – 150.00
    Sugar shaker, 5" T., blue mark #52 .... $110.00 – 150.00
    Sugar shaker, 5" T., green mark #47 .... $110.00 – 150.00
Plate 1177
    Syrup w/underplate, 6" T., green mark #52 .... $160.00 – 200.00
Plate 1178
    Egg warmer, 5½" dia., green mark #47 .... $135.00 – 175.00
    Sugar shaker, 5" T., blue mark #52 .... $150.00 – 200.00
Plate 1179
    Double egg cup, 3½" T., mark #93 .... $50.00 – 70.00
    Single egg cup, 2½" T., mark #93 .... $40.00 – 60.00
Plate 1180
    Egg server, 6¼" W., blue mark #84 .... $135.00 – 160.00
Plate 1181
    Tea tiles, each 5½" W., green mark #47 ....(Each) $70.00 – 90.00

PAGES 228 and 229

Plate 1182
    Creamer and sugar, sugar 7" W., and creamer 6½" W.,
    blue mark #39 .... $160.00 – 200.00
Plate 1183
    Tea strainer, 6" L., unmarked .... $160.00 – 200.00
Plate 1184
    Tea strainer, 6" L., blue mark #52 .... $150.00 – 200.00
    Tea strainer, 6" L., blue mark #52 .... $160.00 – 200.00
Plate 1185
    Individual tea pot, 4¾" T., blue mark #4 .... $75.00 – 100.00
Plate 1186
    Sugar and creamer and matching tray, tray 8¾" L., sugar
    3½" T. and creamer 2½" T., green mark #47 .... $175.00 – 225.00
Plate 1187
    Condensed milk holder w/underplate, 6" T., mark #80...... $125.00 – 175.00
    Condensed milk holder w/underplate, 6" T., green mark
    #47 .... $150.00 – 200.00
Plate 1188
    Basket dish, 7" L., green mark #47................................. $90.00 – 125.00
Plate 1189
    Toast rack, 8¼" L., blue mark #84 .... $120.00 – 160.00
Plate 1190
    Creamer and sugar, 4¾" T., ... $120.00 – 160.00
    Butter dish, 7½" dia., blue mark #52 .... $130.00 – 160.00
Plate 1191
    Shaving mug, 4" T., green mark #47 .... $125.00 – 175.00
Plate 1192
    Serving dish, 8" W., blue mark #84................................. $175.00 – 225.00
Plate 1193
    Mustache cup, blue mark #52.. $275.00 – 325.00
    Mustache cup, green mark #47 .... $175.00 – 225.00
Plate 1194
    Bon bon dish, 5½" W., green mark #47 .... $150.00 – 200.00

PAGES 230 and 231

Plate 1195
    Lamp, 12½" T., mark unknown .... $250.00 – 300.00
Plate 1196
    Flower arranger, 5½" W., 3½" T., blue mark #52 .... $150.00 – 200.00
Plate 1197
    Knife rest, 3½" long, green mark #47 .... $100.00 – 140.00

Plate 1198
Punch cups, 2¾" T., green mark #47 ....(Each) $50.00 – 75.00
Plate 1199
Toothpick holder, 2" T., green mark #47............................ $50.00 – 75.00
Plate 1200
Set of 8 luncheon plates, each 9" W., blue mark #52(Each) $50.00 – 80.00
Plate 1201
Covered jar, 6¼" T., unmarked .... $150.00 – 200.00
Cup, 2½" T., green mark #52 .... $75.00 – 100.00
Syrup w/underplate, 6½" T., green mark #52 .... $135.00 – 175.00
Mug, 4½" T., green mark #52 .... $150.00 – 200.00
Plate 1202
Potpourri jar, 5¾" T., green mark #47............................... $200.00 – 250.00
Plate 1203
Toothpick holder, 2¼" T., green mark #47 .... $75.00 – 100.00
Toothpick holder, 2" T., blue mark #52............................. $75.00 – 100.00
Toothpick holder, 2¾" T., green mark #47 .... $75.00 – 100.00
Toothpick holder, 2¼" T., blue mark #84 .... $75.00 – 100.00
Toothpick holder, 2½" T., green mark #47 .... $75.00 – 100.00
Plate 1204
Sauce dish, underplate and ladle, underplate 5½" long,
green mark #47.. $75.00 – 100.00

Plate 1205
Bell shaped match holder and striker, 3½" T., green mark
#47 .... $150.00 – 200.00
Bell shaped match holder and striker, 3½" T., mark #82,
also has original sticker #53 .... $150.00 – 200.00
Plate 1206
Dish, two-tier, bottom 6" W., top 3" W., blue mark #84...... $50.00 – 75.00

PAGE 232

Plate 1207
Ginger jar, 7½" T., mark #55 .... $250.00 – 350.00
Plate 1208
Mayonnaise set w/underplate and ladle, 7" W., blue mark
#52 .... $175.00 – 225.00
Plate 1209
Milk pitcher, 7" T., green mark #47 .... $250.00   325.00
Plate 1210
Slanted cheese dish, 7½" L., green mark #47 .... $150.00 – 200.00
Condiment dish, 5¼" T., green mark #47 .... $140.00 – 170.00

Schroeder's ANTIQUES Price Guide

. . . is the #1 best-selling antiques & collectibles value guide on the market today, and here's why . . .

8½ x 11, 608 Pages, $12.95

• *More than 300 advisors, well-known dealers, and top-notch collectors work together with our editors to bring you accurate information regarding pricing and identification.*

• *More than 45,000 items in almost 500 categories are listed along with hundreds of sharp original photos that illustrate not only the rare and unusual, but the common, popular collectibles as well.*

• *Each large close-up shot shows important details clearly. Every subject is represented with histories and background information, a feature not found in any of our competitors' publications.*

• *Our editors keep abreast of newly-developing trends, often adding several new categories a year as the need arises.*

If it merits the interest of today's collector, you'll find it in *Schroeder's*. And you can feel confident that the information we publish is up to date and accurate. Our advisors thoroughly check each category to spot inconsistencies, listings that may not be entirely reflective of market dealings, and lines too vague to be of merit. Only the best of the lot remains for publication.

Without doubt, you'll find
SCHROEDER'S ANTIQUES PRICE GUIDE
the only one to buy for
reliable information and values.

COLLECTOR BOOKS
A Division of Schroeder Publishing Co., Inc.